HARRIERS

"Look it up. It's in the dictionary."

- Mike Almond

har·ri·er² (hăŕē-ər)

n.

1. A cross-country runner

Joseph P. Shivers and Paul L. Shivers

Fresh Writers Books

PO Box 82, Uniontown OH 44685

Authors: Joseph P. Shivers and Paul L. Shivers

Publisher: Bill Jelen

PrePress: Fine Grains (India) Private Limited, New Delhi, India.

Cover: Shannon Mattiza, 6'4 Productions

Cover Photo: Nick Cool, TheImageWorksPhotographic.com

Published by: Fresh Writers Books, PO Box 82, Uniontown OH 44685

Distributed by: Independent Publishers Group

First Printing: March 2006. Printed with Revisions in November 2006. Printed in USA

Library of Congress Control Number: 2005939079

ISBN 1-932802-95-9

The events in this book are based on a true story.

About the Authors

Joe Shivers has run cross country for the Salem schools since seventh grade. He kept notes during his sophomore and junior seasons, which the book spans. In Middle School, he excelled in the Power of the Pen writing competition.

Paul Shivers has been running since he was 4 years old and joined the Salem Junior high cross country team in 7th grade.

Paul and Joe were winners in the 2005 Fresh Writers Writing Program. This program encourages high school students to consider literary careers and funds a summer co-op program during which this book was created. For more information about the

Fresh Writers Program, contact
Bill@FreshWritersBooks.com

Dedication

For Grandma

Contents

Chapter 1

●

The Pact

*"We can't all be heroes because someone has to
sit on the curb and clap as they go by."*
                                                    – Will Rogers

Paul got out of the car onto the Northern edge of the Salem
High School parking lot, thanked his father for the ride, and
walked over to the island of grass where his teammates were
already gathered. He could have jogged, but this was his first
day of high school cross country practice, and he wanted to
save his strength. Soon he would have to run two miles. Or
even three.

Paul had run his first race at the age of 4; a quick 200 meter
sprint at the local track. Since then his passion for running had
grown. He was a full year younger than most of his
classmates, and never received a legitimate chance in other
sports to show his talent or develop experience and
confidence. In the summer before his 6th grade year, Paul
began training to run. He was conservative at first, three or
four runs a week, and a road race here or there. By Junior
High, Paul had extended his training into a more rigorous,
demanding schedule with 5 to 7 runs a week including interval
and tempo runs. He was entering high school with high
expectations for himself and for his team.

Most of the boys and girls around him were unfamiliar
upperclassmen: Alex Hoopes, Alex Barnett, Isaac Ieropoli,
Andrew Bender, Jason Naylor, and Jim Dombroski. But as he

---

looked around Paul recognized a few faces he knew from Junior High. Jason Stewart, Tyler Bender, and Andy Thompson were all in Paul's grade, though only Andy had run cross country in junior high. Matt Yanek, another former middle school runner, noticed Paul from under one of the trees that sat on the team's patch of grass.

"Hey Paul. How's it going?" Yanek stood up to greet him. Paul appraised the boy, one grade older but no longer taller than he. Now that they both stood a little under six feet, Paul noticed how much stockier Yanek was than most runners.–he looked more like a wrestler or a football player. Two years ago, when they had both run for the junior high team, he had beaten Paul every race. It was nothing personal, but Paul hated Yanek. Paul accepted nothing less than winning from himself. So, he could not endure losing to anyone, even to the more physically mature Yanek.

"What's up, Matt." Outside of running, Paul (like most people) got along well with the boy. He was well–liked due to his warm personality, and his fellow runners respected him. In conversations with him and about him, his teammates dropped his first name and called him just "Yanek." He negotiated most of life with a smile and a laugh. His laugh, though disarming, was perfunctory, an obligation to be performed before he could continue the conversation. Talking to him, one got the impression that he brought great, infectious enthusiasm to any topic, and he seemed to expect fantastic things to come from the exchange. Nor did he ever seem disappointed when the talk was meaningless or unpleasant. If the subject under discussion made the other parties sad or discouraged, he refocused his energies to fixing their troubles. He could not stand silence and always had a slew of topics at the ready just in case the conversation flagged. If his earnestness made the listeners marvel, he grinned along with them. Today, however, Matt was in a serious mood.

"Nothin'." Yanek's clear blue eyes returned Paul's gaze. Each was still wary of the other. In junior high, Yanek had always won. But when Yanek moved on to high school and Paul continued racing for the junior high team, he had beaten the older boy's best times. Yanek had not expected that. But Yanek did not have Paul's hatred of losing; he tended to live more in the moment. And right now, he had more pressing concerns than his rivalry with Paul. "Do you know anything about this new coach?"

"Not much," Paul replied. "My dad said he was from Marlington. His name's Almond." Paul's father was on the school board, which had hired Almond only a few days earlier. Salem had a strong

While Matt and Paul speculated about the new coach, Paul's cousin Joe talked to some of the other boys on the team.

"We're gonna make you do all kinds o' stuff," one of the upperclassmen informed him.

"Why?" Joe asked. He generally stayed away from belligerent people, and was unused to bullying. He was constantly reading a book or studying for tests or classes, and he did not involve himself in any wrongdoing or arguments. His sense of humor was beyond his age: it took more than the usual high school antics to make him laugh.

"'Cause you're a freshman. You'll be 'Fish.'"

"What? Why would you call me Fish?"

"There has to be a Fish. I was Fish last year," piped in Josh Matthews, a sophomore. Josh's dark eyes glimmered with amusement. Josh Matthews was distinguished mainly by his stature and humor. He stood about five–and–a–half–feet tall and weighed barely over 100 pounds. He wore a constant grin, and he laughed frequently and enthusiastically. Because he so often maintained his easy–come, easy–go demeanor, an electric current was almost palpable when he got serious. He had been on the fringe of the top runners in junior high, but remained inspired enough to continue his running in high school.

"I don't know, Josh," Joe replied. He knew Josh a little already from their days together on the junior high team, when Josh had beaten him consistently. Joe did not especially mind. Like Paul, he was a late–bloomer who had improved significantly since middle school. Unlike Paul, Joe had no expectation of ever being the high school's top runner. He would be lucky to finish among Salem's top seven.

"You don't get a choice, freshman," replied the upperclassman who had begun the discussion. All this talk of seniority was beginning to grate on Joe. Running was the ultimate meritocracy: the fastest seven guys made varsity. It did not matter who was older or who had been on the team longer, honors were accorded based on times.

If Joe had thought about it longer, he might have decided that his teammates cared so much about seniority because they were not very good at actually running. The Salem boys simply were not that fast. But there were exceptions. Robert Vogt, who had graduated last year, inspired Salem runners by qualifying as an individual for the Regional meet. Shane Harding, a senior, was filling Vogt's spikes and looked as though he might be even faster than he. A good cross country team, however, needs more than a single fast runner. Paul was optimistic in his dreams of glory. But he was not alone in them.

It was during their freshman year, in 2001, that Josh Matthews and Matt Yanek had made an agreement, a "pact" they would later call it. They agreed to win a state championship by the end of their education at Salem High School, a short four years to accomplish something so few had in the past. What made their dreams all the more unrealistic was that their team failed to reach the Regional meet that year: Salem was not one of the top 70 out of 185 teams in its division. By 2002, Vogt, the top runner and team leader, had graduated. The talent coming up from the middle school was modest. As freshmen, Yanek ran barely under nineteen minutes in the 5k, and Josh had yet to break twenty. If they had been freshmen girls, their futures would have been bright. As it was, they seemed naïve to think that in three years Salem could climb past 70 teams, let alone defeat proven programs with considerable experience advantages at the State Meet in Columbus. Yanek and Josh were secretive about their pact, keeping it to themselves, but using it as a constant motivator to attain their full potential.

Everyone's eyes turned to the car that had just pulled up: red, shiny, a young man's car. And sure enough, the man who stepped out looked young enough to be in college. He seemed to radiate exuberance through his dark skin, from the soles of his running shoes to his gleaming black high–top. He smiled like someone who never got tired of smiling. And he was the only man the team had ever seen wearing such short shorts after puberty.

"My name is Michael Almond. I'm your new coach." Even his voice was that of a kid. The words came out high and clear.

"I'm 24 years old, I was a 5 time All–American at Malone College, and I'm a Christian. I've been married for just over three years. And I just found out that my wife is four weeks pregnant." So he was young. And a fast runner, to whom a lot of things were happening fast: new job, new team, and new child. It barely occurred to the coach how strange it was for him to mention the news to complete strangers. "We just found out, and you guys are, like, the first people I've told." The honor drew the kids in; evidently Almond cared about them already.

"I grew up in Painesville," Almond continued, "but I've known about Salem for a long time. I was in high school when you guys won the state title in '93, and everybody all across the state knew Salem. And do you guys know Jason Julian?" All of the kids had heard the name, and some knew its significance. Jason Julian was the legendary runner who had captained the State championship team, who still held the school record of 15:53. He made even Robert Vogt and Shane Harding look slow. They knew Jason Julian.

Julian was only one of the great athletes Salem had graduated over the years: others included three NFL players and Jenni Brown, a cross country runner who still holds statewide records. Salem High School had been, at various times, a powerhouse in one or more sports.

SHS is 25 miles south of Youngstown in the northern tip of Columbiana County, and as part of the job–rich Mahoning Valley, the school graduating class reached a peak of 325 students in 1975. Major college recruiters came to see Quaker athletes compete against the biggest and best teams in the state. But over the years, as industries closed and manufacturing jobs disappeared, students disappeared from Salem's schools. And as SHS hallways emptied, the athletic talent pool drained, and Salem slid into mediocrity. With the school's population dwindling, the Quakers dropped to lower divisions in many sports

"I raced against Julian at Regionals my sophomore year. He was a senior, and everybody thought he was gonna win it. It was at the Boardman course, the same place they hold your Regionals now. It was an insanely cold day. I'm not kidding you; there was three inches of snow on the ground. I mean, it was *cold*.

"Well I beat him, and I won the meet. When the official gave him his second–place medal, Julian took it and threw it on the ground." Some of the more knowledgeable runners were realizing exactly how fast this meant their new coach was. Their respect for him was increasing with each word.

"And my coach at Malone always talked about what a great booster program you have here, and what a great tradition you guys have. So I know about Salem, and I'm glad to be here." The booster program he mentioned was the X–tra Mile Club, an organization made up of parents of track and cross country runners.

"I want to take this team back to where it was in 1993. My ultimate goal is for us to win a state championship, and for Salem to go to state every year. I don't know about this year yet, because we're starting practices so late." Late? The first race wasn't for nearly a month. "All the good teams start in early June. That's when we'll start next year. Really, you guys should be running all year. I don't want a bunch of kids who play other sports that are doing cross country 'to stay in shape.' I want you to be committed to running. Because I want Salem to be the best."

This was the coach Paul, Matt, and Josh had been hoping for. Almond had seen success, and he wanted to show it to all of them. He was holding them to the standards of the Salem he had known, the Salem of ten years ago. But Paul also had his concerns. Never before had he run so many miles in a day or week. Never before had he run every day of the week. He did not like being told to quit basketball, his sport of choice. Ultimately Paul feared change and the unknown. He was a freshman used to the sheltered world of junior high and uncompetitive junior high sports. All of a sudden he had been thrust into a situation with new people who presented Paul with seemingly revolutionary ideas. The only thing that calmed Paul was his will to win, since that was oftentimes all that mattered to him.

"All right, that's the end of my speech. There won't be many more of those; I'm not really much of a talker." Of all the predictions he made that day, this one eventually proved least true.

"Oh, there's one more thing I've gotta tell you guys, just 'cause it was so weird. My dog gave birth yesterday." The juxtaposition of this pregnancy story with his wife's did not seem to strike him as the least bit odd. "And it did it all over our new white carpet. So all the afterbirth and blood and everything was sitting there. My wife and I just moved into our house, and we were like, 'Oh, no, we'll have to clean it all up. It's gonna stain.' But then the dog started eating it and licking the blood up. I guess it's like an adaptation from the wild, so the smell doesn't attract predators. When she was done, the carpet was spotless."

The boys and girls listened with mingled disgust and interest. Almond told the story with the same language any of them would have, and with a sense of wonder befitting a teenager. Joe felt drawn to the new coach, and he wondered whether the unconventional anecdote had been intended as an icebreaker. As the runners learned more about him, they still found it hard to guess the reasons behind many of his actions. Whether he had hoped to break the tension of his arrival or only to tell a cool story, Almond made a strong impression on the high schoolers sitting in front of him. It was hard not to form some kind of opinion about somebody after he gives a graphic description of animals being born on his rug.

Of course, not everyone liked Almond. The new coach often came off as abrasive: even though he was a newcomer, he made next to no effort at diplomacy. He was especially brusque with kids who he did not think were committed enough to running. His demands and his personality became too much for some of the students who set off on the road with him that day. But several stuck around, and kept running.

That year, 2002, both the girls and boys teams finished well enough in the district championships ("Districts," as the runners called it) to qualify for the Regional Meet ("Regionals"). Despite a knee injury, Paul finished third on the team at Districts with a personal record (P.R.) of eighteen minutes, three seconds. Joe also set a P.R.; his time of 19:18 placed him sixth among the Quakers. Both of them, and the team as a whole, performed much worse the next week at Regionals. Although it finished dead–last in that race, the Salem boys cross country team had not enjoyed so much success since 1993.

Senior captain Shane Harding ran well enough at Regionals to advance to the 2002 State Meet as an individual. Many of the underclassmen traveled to Columbus to watch Shane's race, in which he narrowly missed earning All–Ohio status. After seeing the race, the Quakers wanted even more to qualify for State next year. The 2003 team would be relatively inexperienced. The only returning upperclassman was Jason Naylor, the rest would be juniors (Yanek and Matthews) and sophomores (the Shiverses, Jason Stewart, and Andy Thompson). Almond's success as a coach would rely heavily on these runners, and theirs on him.

On October 18, 2003, the Salem Quakers Cross Country team lined up alongside eighteen other teams at the Trumbull County Fairgrounds to compete for the Ohio High School Athletic Association (OHSAA) Northeast District Championship. The team's goal was to finish among the top four teams in that race and qualify for the Regional meet, one step closer to a berth in the State meet. The runners stared down the horse racing track that constituted the first few hundred meters of the course, and they focused on the dimly–lit stable through which the course ran. Anxiousness shone on all seven of the Salem runners' faces, but confidence dominated their thoughts. Their view shifted to the official, dressed in the standard navy blue OHSAA jacket, standing on a step ladder as he called the runners to their marks. He raised his starter pistol, paused, and then pulled the trigger. At the explosion, all 134 runners broke toward the stable, falling into one giant pack. Salem had begun its mission: to prove that a relatively small school just two years into a new program could compete at the State level.

The crowd, seated in the horse track grandstands, erupted into cheers as the race began. From the gun, Patrick Gorby took off in an attempt to latch onto the lead pack. His form was nearly perfect; he had a slight forward lean and an efficient arm carriage. He was a lithe 5'8", 110 with coarse black hair and a long forehead. Patrick appeared effortless as he sprinted to the front of the race; his face would remain stoic and his breathing light throughout the race. Though only a freshman, he had beaten everyone on the team in all but two races this season. What set him apart from was not a higher level of dedication, but an "I must win" attitude. He believed that he was the best, and if he fell short, he could always rationalize it and preserve his self–confidence.

At the beginning of the year, Patrick was the dark horse of the team. He was a freshman coming off a spectacular eighth grade year, but no one knew what to expect from him. Gorby had excessive amounts of energy, constantly bugged the upperclassmen, and did not take well to misbehavior or pranks. He was persuaded to run track as a seventh grader and soon found just how good he was. In his first high school meet, he astonished everyone by placing second overall and leading the team. Over the course of the year he had surrendered his top spot only twice and continued to amaze his teammates and coaches

Gorby took the lead, with a front–running style derived from his hero, Steve Prefontaine. He led his competition down the initial straightaway, into an empty stable. After passing through the building, the course ran several hundred meters to the opposite side of the fairgrounds. From there, it wove through rows of stables and made a quick loop around a lightly wooded area. Finally, the path extended back to the grandstands, where it led back toward the starting line. Then the loop repeated itself, returned to the horse track, and broke off into a finish line. Gorby visualized the remainder of the course as he slowed to his "race pace." Following closely behind him was Aiman Scullion, Almond's first recruit.

If one got to know Aiman, he was the cockiest, most arrogant person anyone would ever care to meet. But he disguised this astonishingly well with meek and humble manners. His father was a Salem grad who traveled abroad after high school. He met Aiman's mother in Africa, and soon thereafter was

Chapter 1- The Pact

married to her. Aiman was born in Morocco and raised there; he made the trip to America in fourth grade. He had short curly hair and stood 6'3". His body had developed at a constant pace; he had been relatively short in junior high. He was a thin 135 and appeared to be even lighter.

His first love was soccer. Because of his commitment to that sport, Aiman had not run his freshman year, though he had been a top–5 runner in 8th grade (when soccer had not been offered as a school sport). His training that year was shaky, and he failed to beat Paul once. During their freshman year of track, Paul received all the attention from the track coach. Aiman was largely ignored, despite his blooming talent. His body was finally developing into an ideal running frame, and he had natural endurance to back it up. Almond nearly gave up on Aiman after he failed to break 11 minutes in the 3200 meter run that year, but the coach succeeded in recruiting him for the 2003 Cross Country season. Aiman did not quit soccer, however. Under Salem rules, he could play two sports in the same season, but had to declare a primary sport. Aiman chose soccer, so he had to attend every soccer game and practice – a price he readily paid for the sport he loved. He did not necessarily *like* running, in contrast. But he desperately wanted to win, to be the best at something, and soccer just was not offering him that.

He got off to an impressive start in the 2003 season, opening under 17:30 and placing second on the team. It was the first cross country race in which he had ever beaten Paul, and his confidence was buoyed. Playing two sports soon caught up with him, however, and he went into a midseason slump. Now that his mileage was tapered down and his workouts were scheduled around soccer games, he was ready for a breakout performance in the tournaments.

Opening characteristically slowly was Paul, who steadily progressed through the pack as it traversed the dirt floor of the stable. Paul thrived on blowing by runners throughout the race, and he started the race near last place. Once he had a sense of how his body was handling the pace, he could adjust and move up to the front. Today he was exaggerating this strategy so that he might run with even splits – that is, run each of the race's three miles in the same amount of time. As he ignited a surge around a crowd he noticed his teammate, Ryan Griffith, who had displayed his inexperience in the sport by opening with the leaders. Now, he was falling back to the middle of the field. Ryan's boyish face turned briefly as Paul passed, then focused back on the path ahead.

Ryan showed up for his first run in early August of 2003, on the first day of mandatory practice. The team had already been practicing together all summer, and no one had expected any newcomers so close to the start of the official season. The shoes he wore, Converse, revealed his total ignorance of the sport. His cargo shorts, heavy t–shirt, and stunt bike exemplified everything a runner should not have. But despite his weighty clothes and clunky shoes, he hung on through that run, a seven–mile workout. He came back, too, and became as much a part of the team as those who had been there for two months. His playful personality paralleled Gorby's, and the two got along quite well. He did not delve too deeply into the sport early on, but he soon noticed he was fighting for a varsity spot. His gradual improvement put him among the team's top seven by the end of the season, and Almond selected him to represent Salem in the District meet.

Shortly after surpassing Ryan, Paul moved past Joe. At six feet and 140 pounds, Joe was the same height as his cousin, and slightly heavier. He usually finished a minute or so behind Paul, who now moved forward toward the next pack of runners. Joe barely noticed as Paul disappeared from view: he was having the race of his life.

Joe had been sixth man on the Salem team for most of the 2003 season, but in the two races before Districts he had lost his spot. At the Metro Athletic Conference (MAC) Championship meet, senior Jason Naylor had beaten him. The week before Districts, Joe had lost to Ryan Griffith and Josh

Matthews at the Sim Earich Invitational. Sim Earich, like Districts, was held at the Trumbull County Fairgrounds. That race was the worst of Joe's season, and it shook Almond's confidence in him. The coach let Joe run varsity at Districts under one condition: if Joe ran a third bad race in a row, Almond would replace him with Jason Naylor for the rest of the postseason.

Joe had never run a race under as much pressure as was on him today at Districts. In the morning, hours before the race, anxiety had almost paralyzed him. Then after the team's warm–up jog, fifteen minutes before the race, he had gained an inexplicable confidence. Joe felt an absolute certainty that he would earn the right to keep his varsity spot. All he had to do was beat Ryan, as he had in every race but Sim Earich. Cross country was the easiest sport in the world, he thought. When Paul passed him 400 yards into the race, Joe was already practically celebrating. The next two–plus miles would be his victory lap.

Paul continued his assault on the now strung–out pack as they made the first turn and began the nearly half–mile straightaway. He jumped to the outside, into the thicker, unmowed grass spotted with spectators to pass the many runners still ahead of him. As he moved out of the horserace track and onto a gravel path he overcame yet another teammate, the capricious Mike Overholser.

Mike was a former wrestler who had been recruited for cross country by Andy Thompson, who himself played both sports. Mike stood 5'8'', with naturally tan skin and coarse brown hair. He joined the team in the summer but rarely came to practice. Just when he was showing signs of improvement, he disappeared. No one knew exactly where he was: whether on vacation, out of town with relatives, or just not at practice. When camp rolled around in August, Mike reappeared, and in better shape than Almond or anyone else had imagined. Perhaps because of his limited summer training, Mike never had a breakout race, though he maintained a top–5 spot throughout the year. The team was relying on him to boost them among the elite teams, but too often he seemed uninterested in running – sometimes even during races. Mike Overholser was a blister for Almond, causing frequent pain and requiring constant attention; the boy's fiery personality sparked many arguments, and forcing him to attend practice had been a summer–long struggle. But his talent could not be overlooked, and Almond made it a priority to bring out Mike's full potential.

After a dizzying maze of turns around stables and paddocks, Paul crossed the first mile in a decent time of 5:25. He was on pace for under 17, but, more importantly, he had not killed himself to hit his goal time in the first third of the race. By now he had passed dozens of competitors and four teammates–Matt Yanek, Mike Overholser, Joe Shivers, and Ryan Griffith. As Paul picked off runner after runner, Jason Naylor, the alternate, and Josh Matthews, who had not qualified for varsity, stood screaming their encouragement. Matthews had put in the miles, the time, and the effort to be a varsity runner, but simply had not run the solid late season races Ryan had. Almond chose the senior, Jason, as alternate over Matthews because Jason had a faster P.R., and in the event of an injury or poor performance by a top–seven runner, Jason would have a better chance of providing the team with a worthy performance. Despite the setback, Josh stayed true to his team and showed up at the meet. His teammates respected him for that.

At the start of the second lap, Paul, for the first time all season, caught and passed Patrick, who was now fading. The freshman's opening sprint to the front had cost him a lot of energy, and he now looked as if he were running through sand. Mike and Yanek, a way back, fell into stride with each other and would maintain a connection the rest of the race. Paul, now on the long straightaway for the second time, caught sight of Aiman about a hundred meters ahead of him. He crossed the two–mile–mark in 10:55 and continued towards Aiman.

By the end of the stretch, they were running together until, finally, Paul made a move with 1000 meters to go, around what had been the first mile mark. His adrenaline was up; he began a surge to the finish and a possible sub–17 minute 5k. He remembered Almond asking him "What are you going to run today, Paul?" and replying "I'm going to run a 16:55 today; this course is fast." Almond had grinned at Paul's predictions, as he had run 17:21 the previous week on the same course.

The crowd's roar grew exponentially louder in Paul's ears as he closed towards the race track and the finish line. It reached its peak as he rounded the corner of the grandstands and stepped onto the raked dirt track. Only two runners had held off his powerful 3rd mile; they finished out of reach of Paul's limited sprinting speed. Paul began kicking towards the finish with all of his remaining energy. As he crossed the finish line, his arms went limp and he stumbled through the chute. Seconds later, he turned to see Gorby finishing, followed closely by Aiman. They exchanged high fives and words of congratulations as they waited for the remainder of their team. Many runners later, Matt and Mike finished. The team concluded with Joe some 30 seconds behind them and Ryan a few seconds later.

The team gathered in a remote area of the grandstands. Since they had not all seen each other finish, the Quakers reported on their times and places. Paul had managed to run his 16:55, proving his coach wrong and taking 3rd place. Patrick was right behind him in fifth with a 17:03. The freshman hardly acknowledged that Paul had beaten him; as soon as the race was over he began complaining of a knee injury that had not existed until that moment. Right behind Gorby, Aiman placed sixth in 17:05. Likewise, Matt and Mike were within seconds of each other at 17:37 and 17:43, respectively. They finished 22nd and 27th in the race, which put Salem's score at 60 points. This total was calculated by assigning Salem one point for the finishing spot of each of the top five runners, disregarding the finishes of runners who did not have five–man teams. Thus Yanek scored only 21 points; the race was scored as if one of the boys in front of him (a boy with only two teammates) had not run.

Almond jogged up to his runners. "Guys, that was awesome!"

"Did we win, Coach?" Paul asked, still short of breath.

"I don't know," Almond replied. "It's gonna be close between us and Mooney." Cardinal Mooney, a Catholic school in Youngstown, had five solid runners including the meet champion, Colin Durina. While the boys waited for the officials to process the results, they headed back to the team's tent. They grabbed some of the snacks that the X–tra Mile Club had provided, and their parents and teammates congratulated them. Jason Naylor, Josh Matthews, Lance Murphy, Andy Thompson, Jason Stewart, and Tommy Yuhaniak gave them high–fives and "good jobs." Paul, despite "P.R.–ing" and leading the team for the first time since Junior High, was not ready to celebrate the race yet – he was waiting to learn if the team had won. It mattered little; Salem was on its way to Regionals whether it finished first or second in the District. But Paul still wanted to win.

The results soon came in, showing that the race was indeed close: a tie, in fact. Salem and Cardinal Mooney both scored 60 points, so the officials went to a tie–breaker: the finishing places of the two teams' respective sixth runners. Joe's 18:18 beat the sixth Mooney runner's time to seal the meet, and Salem was crowned District Champion.

Almond shouted over the cheering boys and girls that swarmed Joe, "Didn't I tell you just the other day how important each runner is to the team? Ties happen all the time in tournament meets."

Chapter 2

The Rivals

"The moment of victory is much too short to live for that and nothing else."

– Martina Navratilova

Most cross country runners perceive that the outside world does not care about their sport. Beyond the casual congratulations from a teacher or neighbor, success generally goes unnoticed. They can run through miles of stinging rain to win a meet, but they'll still get less newspaper ink than the local football team that lost its third game in a row. The day can be beautiful, but most potential spectators would rather spend Saturday morning sleeping in than standing around watching a race. For a community to be moderately interested in its cross country team, other sports must not exist in the school district. Some smaller schools that can't afford football teams have more than half of their graduating classes involved in cross country and a whole town behind them. But in large schools in Ohio, football and basketball seem to dominate the town's attention.

In this setting, many runners develop attitudes. In their early years, they work up a dislike for all football players, who pick on them for being skinny and for running without being forced to by a coach as a means of punishment. Some runners decide that the crumbs of glory they could taste aren't worth months of preparation and sacrifice, don't dedicate their full energy or time, and ultimately suffer for it in races. In social situations, many yield to the traditional jocks as social superiors. These timid runners enjoy their sport because it gives them a chance to escape from mainstream high school society and revel in cross country's obscurity.

But some runners decide they don't need the world's approval (or its notice, for that matter). These are the teammates who huddle together against their cold, apathetic environment and care about their sport. These are the ones who become great. Ironically, these are the only teams of which the world takes note. The Salem runners knew that their opportunity was there, an opportunity to be recognized among the football, basketball, and baseball teams, if they could make it to State.

"Guys, we are a shoe–in for the State Meet. All you need to do is get up on Saturday morning, run, and we'll go home with a one–way ticket to Scioto Downs," Almond would say with increasing frequency. "And I'm not just telling you this based on a hunch. I've crunched the numbers and done the calculations. I've been around this sport for over 10 years now. I've taken results from each of the 24 Regional– qualifying teams and scored the meet. The only way we won't qualify for State is if all of our top 5 run poorly. And there is no way that is going to happen, we are peaking ! This is where we fly, where we get excited and beat people. We could place as high as second; St. V's isn't that great. To prove how confident I am in you guys, I've booked the hotel rooms in Columbus for both the boys' and the girls' teams." The confidence generated by his actions spread fluidly throughout the team. The downside to their secure demeanor was that many of the boys became careless; they lost focus and began planning on the State meet for which they had yet to qualify.

The Ohio High School Athletic Association, a non–profit organization founded in 1906, controls over twenty statewide tournaments. The OHSAA assigns high school cross country teams into three divisions based on the number of ninth, tenth, and eleventh graders of each gender enrolled in a school the previous year. Salem's girls and boys teams both belonged to Division II, among schools smaller than those in Division I but bigger than the schools in D III. Each division's state championship race draws runners from four regions across the state; each region, in turn, is split into several districts. The requirements for entering the State Meet vary from Region to Region, from year to year.

In 2003, Salem needed to be in the top half dozen teams from the Northeast Region in order to move on. In addition to the six teams that would qualify, so would the individual runners who placed among the top twenty–four in the Region. While Aiman, Paul, and Patrick had a shot at qualifying this way, they viewed individual qualifier status as just that–status. They were confident that they would make the trip with the team; any individual success they might enjoy as underclassmen racing against the top runners in the state for the first time was a bonus.

Despite Almond's optimism, the team still murmured about the region's top teams. Paul had done his research and presented some of the information to the team throughout the week leading up to the race. "Obviously, Edgewood is the team to beat. I don't see them losing to anyone in our region," Paul said, quickly eliminating a 1st place finish as a possibility. Ashtabula Edgewood had been ranked number 1 in the polls all year, and never even came close to losing a meet. Their team had no outstanding frontrunner, but a solid 1 through 5 that no other team could match. "Then we have the poll's number 2 team, Akron St. Vincent St. Mary's. Besides Lebron James going there, they have a great team. Their top guy, Matt Buzek, is probably gonna win State. He wins every race, so he only scores one point. It's like St. V's scores only four runners."

"I love to beat those Catholic schools," Almond told them whenever Mooney or St. V's came up in conversation, "they can recruit all they want and get an unfair advantage, but we're still going to beat them." Paul and Joe were both Catholics but understood that Almond wasn't attacking religious schools, just that religious schools could recruit.

"I think the dark horse for the race is University School. They've gone under the radar all year, but they split their team into two teams at Sim Earich and ran very well," Paul mentioned, noting that any team could come in and run a spectacular race and prevent a favorite from qualifying. "We've seen all these teams this year, but I'm not too worried about them. If we can just beat Mooney again, we should be all right."

The two schools were similarly sized, though Mooney was able to draw runners from school districts around Youngstown because it was a private school. Almond prided his team on beating private schools because they held this advantage, and Salem's runners used Mooney's superior position to motivate themselves. So far Mooney's boys hadn't bested the Quakers, and they'd had three chances. Almond's team knew that Mooney had a chance of advancing to State, but they did not want to let Mooney do it by beating Salem.

The two team's first meeting had been the third week of the season at the East Palestine Invitational. Salem won the meet, defeating Mooney by a mere six points. The next race between them had come in the last meet of the regular season, at the Sim Earich Invitational. Salem had easily beaten Mooney that day, running almost 30 points ahead. Mooney came back to the Trumbull County Fairgrounds a week later at Districts, and despite the team's two very different styles, tied Salem only to lose in the tiebreaker. Mooney's number–one runner, sophomore Colin Durina, was the district champion. Behind him were solid 2 through 5 runners. Salem, on the other hand, threw the best one–two–three punch in the state. What hurt the Quakers were relatively weak fourth and fifth runners, and the enormous gap between the two groups. In cross country meets, especially the larger ones where almost every second means another finisher and another point, the first–through–fifth–runner time spread is very important. Salem's was long: almost one minute.

The Quakers ran only light workouts the week before Regionals. The plan was to peak every runner for the race of their lives in order to qualify for State. The weekly mileage that had spiked at 48 dropped to under twenty, less than three miles a day. On Monday the team ran down to Salem's track at Reilly Stadium for a mile time trial, and then ran back, stretched and went home. That was far from difficult compared to the ten milers and intervals they had done since the summer. The rest of the week consisted of short two– or three–mile jogs, a "long day" of four miles, and some striders (short sprints) on Wednesday.

Of course, all of the coach's efforts to prepare the boys to be State qualifiers could not prevent them from also being boys. Despite Almond's increasingly frequent and increasingly desperate pleas that the Quakers take no risks with their bodies, Patrick Gorby had continued his hobby of riding a four–wheeler on the trails near his house. He had never crashed all year, until he had wrecked and hurt his ankle this week. All he could say in his defense was that the ramp had broken; it had not really been his fault. Of course, now he and his teammates would have to endure his injury, even if it increased his 5k time by only a second.

Meanwhile, Aiman had spent the week feuding with the girls' team, and Kimberly "Berly" Kenst in particular. They had traded blows by defacing each other's lawns at night, so the victim had to wake up to a yard full of shaving cream or garbage. Thursday morning Aiman's binder was missing, and he immediately blamed Berly. He spent the day fuming, and when Almond called the boys together after school, the lanky soccer player refused to come.

"Girls, go run." Almond commanded. If Aiman had an issue, then he could discuss it with the team – the boys' team, not necessarily the girls, too. Although Almond coached both, and both girls and guys met under the same tree at the same time everyday, the two teams were autonomous. If one of the boys had a bad race or a bad week of training, he turned to the other guys for reassurance. Almond intended for each team to support its members, even if the person in question wanted no help.

"Aiman," Almond yelled from the circle where he stood with the other seven boys, "If you don't get over here right now you're off the team."

"Okay," replied Aiman without flinching, as if to ask whether Almond would really suspend one of his best runners on the day before Regionals. Not that Aiman's attitude would necessarily have changed, he could be insanely stubborn. The bull–headedness was also one of his greatest advantages: it took a lot of will to practice for two sports everyday, and to travel directly from a meet to a varsity soccer game. But today it meant that Almond had to cajole him over to the team meeting. Eventually Aiman relaxed enough to sit through Almond's talk.

On Friday, the day before the meet, Salem jogged down to Memorial Park, only a half–mile from the high school, and had a pre–race meeting. The plan was, as Almond pointed out, simply to get the blood moving. There the coach gave his last bit of inspiration, for tomorrow he would be far too nervous to orate at his best. What is more, long, elaborate speeches were not appropriate immediately before races; words are insufficient to carry a runner through 3.1 miles of agony. The day before was the time for reasonable talking, the kind that soothes and smoothes the nerves.

Almond assured them that nothing could prevent their going to State; it was a matter of destiny. He, as did the eight boys still in training, called this meet simply "State": not "The State Meet," or "The State Championships," just State. It was shorter, faster, and vaguer, not limited to a cross country race. "State" was a paradise, where everyone who'd ever participated in the sport wanted to go. Almond likened it to a promised land that the team would be rewarded with after months of diligent training and dedication. He had preached all year about State and convinced the team it was the place to be. Paul went home that night, and went to bed earlier than necessary. But he didn't fall asleep at first, because the race dominated his thoughts and fought off his need for rest. Finally, though, he dozed off, with hopes of glory for the following day.

Joe woke up at 9:15 Saturday morning. This was later than usual; on any other week he'd already be on a school bus heading for competition. Most meeets began in the morning, around nine o'clock. But today's meet differed from these others in many ways. By coincidence, October 25 was also the day of the ACT, so Regionals started late in deference to any students who had to race and take the test. And once the Regional Meet got going, it moved slowly. Nearly every cross country meet includes multiple races: boys and girls; Divisions I, II, and III; varsity and "open". Usually meet directors allow thirty minutes for each race, but to ensure that they could all start on time, the Regional races were less frequent. Most importantly, the stakes at Regionals were higher. In a midseason meet, the teams' performances would be less important and their focus could be less than absolute. But Almond didn't want the teams sitting around the course worrying or lazing. Everyone needed to be sharp. So the girls and boys, who usually rode a bus together, traveled separately. The girls, whose race would begin at 11:50, would leave Salem at 10 A.M. But the boys were to remain in Salem for hours, their routines jolted. Joe hadn't slept so late on a Saturday in over two months, but he didn't see any reason to wake up early and loaf around the house.

Paul enjoyed his extra sleep, but as soon as he awoke at 8:30 he was too excited to fall back to sleep. He had one of the strongest stomachs on the team, and always ate a decent breakfast the day of a race. Otherwise, he would face hypoglycemia, which had been a problem for him before he found an adequate eating routine. Joe, on the other hand, ate only a bagel and a banana. Almond had always advised that the team eat nothing big within three hours of a race, and Joe scrupulously adhered to this suggestion. Paul occasionally snacked on pretzels or gagged down a PowerGel Joe considered eating later to be heresy, and he was always troubled when someone nibbled animal crackers an hour before the gun went off. This view was characteristic of Joe's approach to his sport: follow the letter of the law. Never mind that the pretzel–eaters never cramped or vomited, never mind that Almond had meant his recommendation as only a guideline, Joe would obey. His rigid ways comforted and assured him that he was doing right – it was easier than thinking things through himself. Paul listened to every word his coach said, interpreted, and threw in some adjustments. Not every runner is exactly the same after all.

Almond's advice was still sound if interpreted literally; nothing a runner eats on the morning of a race can help him much anyway. The idea behind a meal was to keep from feeling famished, not to energize oneself for a race. The body's glycogen stores are already complete on race day; everything that a runner will spend in the race has already been deposited.

Joe read the local paper over breakfast to occupy his mind. He was as anxious as he'd ever been. He felt as though the strain on him was too great, and that if he thought too long about the importance of this day he would vaporize. No, he would save those thoughts for closer to the race. It wouldn't do to get too excited too early.

So, he tried to distract himself with neutral activities: walking down the block, sketching a still–life in his dining room, and reading a book by George Carlin. Though he'd been running cross country for four years and had witnessed Salem's metamorphosis into a competitive team, he felt as though he didn't understand the sport. His mental preparedness dictated how he performed, but Joe found this nearly impossible to regulate. Almond talked about "caging the lion," saving one's adrenalin for when it mattered. Joe put a great deal of energy into caging this metaphorical lion – if not domesticating it.

Shortly before noon his mother drove him to the high school parking lot, near the tree under which the teams had first seen Almond. It was here also that they convened every day for practice, and whence they always departed for meets. In this respect the arrangement was normal. But otherwise matters were different. The girls' team was not here; they had left for Boardman two hours ago and were now beginning their race. Few members of the boys' team were present at SHS – only the alternate and the seven runners rode the bus during the tournament season. Another variation was the absence of Almond, who was already at the meet to prepare the girls. Sent to supervise the boys was Assistant Coach Russ Hopple.

Hopple, as the boys called him, was essential to the team's functioning. He did the legwork: recording times and places throughout races, measuring training loops with his car, and otherwise helping wherever he could. He was stocky for a runner, and his career hadn't been as successful as Almond's, but he had still run in college (at West Liberty State) and gained valuable knowledge about running. Hopple was more of a friend to the boys than Coach Almond was. Almond seemed aloof – for one, none of the boys could beat him in a race. But Hopple ran workouts with them, engaged in light conversation, and presented an all–around warmer front than the sometimes aloof Almond. He'd come back from the Regional meet just before the girls Division II race was set to go off.

The pre–meet bus rides were always quiet; the shortage of people on the bus made today's more so. The runners were especially withdrawn now. No jokes or conversation interrupted the bus' rumbling. Everyone on board was preparing for the race, fine–tuning his mind. Paul was still brimming with confidence from his spectacular District performance. In order to continue racing well, he thought, he had to utilize the same strategy that he had in the previous meet. He planned to start off slow, get a feel for the race, and then assault the leaders. Certainly he would be top ten in the race, if not top seven (first team all–regional). Qualifying individually required a top twenty–four finish, which Paul took for granted.

Mike Overholser, the rookie, sighed as he planned his own race. He turned to Paul from across the aisle of the bus. "Man," he said, "my last three races I've done terrible." Usually he affected bravado, but he had never run under external pressure, and he was worried. Mike knew he and Matt Yanek would unquestionably make or break the team that day.

So did Paul. "You've just gotta go out slower," Paul told him. "Everybody sprints the first four hundred and kills himself. If you just start at an even pace, you get used to the race. You'll be at the same time at the mile, but you'll feel a ton better."

Mike raised his eyebrows. "Yeah?"

"Think about it," Paul replied. He was confident in the strategy that had taken him to first place on the team at Districts. It was so simple, but nobody seemed to consider it. "You don't even have to try for the first half mile. Just go out in the first hundred meters with me, and then maintain the pace. We'll start way back, but we'll pass like a million people during the race. It really boosts your confidence."

"All right," said Mike, warming up to the idea. Some color returned to his face, and a cocky smile started to play at his lips. "Yeah, Paul. I'll just stick with you, and then I'll out–kick you in the last 400."

Paul chuckled. He was not intimidated at all, but he was glad to see Mike get some of his attitude back. He turned back toward the window, resumed his own strategizing, and slipped on his headphones. Paul would listen to the same CD before his races, in an attempt to settle his nerves and focus on the race.

All the runners on the bus wore headphones plugged into CD players, each with his idiosyncratic psych–up songs. Mike, Matt, Paul, and Naylor all used punk and alternative rock to pump their blood. Ryan and Aiman preferred hip–hop and soft rap, respectively. Joe had immersed himself in this practice only last week, but his success then convinced him to continue it now. His CD was a mix of Oldies that his father had compiled: "C.C. Rider," "Alley–Oop," and "Let's Go." Any kind of music could work: anything that focused the mind and stimulated the adrenal glands.

The entire team broke from their reverie when Boardman High School came into view and the bus slowed to park. They had all seen the course there before; this year Salem had competed in two meets there and the boys who had run in junior high had plenty of experience with the course. But these meets had been early, free of consequences. Today this course would host the most important race of their season.

As they stepped off the bus, the Quakers smiled and joked. Regionals was a fun, exciting time, after all. Several of the boys sported homemade sweatshirts imprinted with a picture of freshman Tommy Yuhaniak. These sweatshirts were the latest and most tangible jokes that targeted Tommy, whose stammering and timidity never failed to amuse some of his teammates. Matt, Mike and Aiman had made them the night before by ironing a photo of a post–race Tommy onto gray hooded sweatshirts. Joe disagreed with the idea; he thought such attire was insulting to Tommy and, more practically, detracted from the seriousness of the race. Paul wanted to know why he had not been in on the latest team activity and demanded a sweatshirt be made for him by the next school day. Either way the shirts were soon off; it was a hot day for late October.

The boys made their way down to the team's tent. They soon picked out its red and black from the dozens of primary–colored camps where other teams gathered. They knew where to look; the tent was in the same place it had been earlier in the year. Almond had stressed to them the importance of doing everything the same way they had all year: no shaving their heads, wearing costumes to the meet, or changing their pre–race routines. No one even needed to faster than usual. Sure

---

enough, the tent was exactly where the boys had expected it to be. But its occupants were startling.

The girls team drifted around, headed nowhere. The girls had just learned the results of their own race. They had failed to advance to the State meet. That news shook the boys. All year Almond had talked about both teams making it to State, together. Although the two teams were separate, a bond did exist between them. The boys and girls had met together for practice, attended the same meets, gone to the same social events, even (though Almond despised it) dated at times. Almond had insisted that both teams could and would go to State; the girls even seemed to have had a better chance. Could Almond have been wrong? Could the boys' season be within hours of ending too?

Before the boys could ponder these melancholy questions long, an agitated Almond appeared.

"Guys, take your stuff and follow me," he ordered. He began walking toward a patch of woods downhill from the tent. The runners looked at each other to see if any of them knew what Almond was thinking. "I don't want the girls' attitudes dragging you guys down."

So the Quakers followed him, set their bags down in a clearing, and lay down to conserve their strength. The day's timetable didn't leave the boys in the shade for long, after a few minutes they got to their feet to warm up for the race. They didn't have to run very far before the sun and dry air brought sheens to their skin. The warm–up run was crucial, even on hotter days than this. The runners had to be ready at the line, for there was no time in the race to waste stretching out their legs. The previous year at this meet there had been a mix of snow and rain, and the temperature had peaked at 40. Almond had told stories about the Regional meet his sophomore year, when two inches of snow had covered the course. On an ideal day the temperature would be around 50 degrees, with clouds blotting out the strength–sapping sun. But today it was close to 75 degrees with the sun gleaming down from the cloudless sky onto the soccer fields, baseball diamonds, and mulch–covered trails.

The Quakers jogged over to the starting line, which lay parallel to a road leading into the heart of Boardman. The line easily fit fifty teams, though today it would need to accommodate only twenty–four in each race.

"What is this?" asked Gorby as the boys set off onto the course. "Do they ever move these soccer goals?" The practice soccer fields that made up the opening straightaway were still set up.

"That's right," chirped Mike. "what kind of loser would ever play soccer. It's gotta be the dumbest sport ever invented." Aiman ignored the obvious provocation.

"We'll just have to avoid those," Paul told them. Everyone knew that, of course; they had all run the course before. But talking about it assured Paul that he himself knew what to do at each hill and turn. Besides that, it filled the tense silence.

"We want to aim for that telephone pole," Paul continued as the boys made their way up a 200 meter climb. "Positioning is key around that first left turn: you don't want to be too far to the outside, but if you're on the inside you'll get boxed in and have to walk." They passed another bottleneck a few hundred meters later, where the course ran between a fenced–off electric house and a tree a few yards away. Then the course followed another fence around a baseball field.

"This is the only real hill on the course," Paul said as the Quakers approached a short, steep, incline. "Don't go crazy up it; just maintain even effort. At the top everyone's going to be dying, and then you can make your move on the downhill." The long slope lasted through a corridor of spectators to the mile–mark, and soon the boys found themselves running along the starting line. Now they passed into the woods where they had camped earlier.

"Okay, the whole course is basically two big loops. The second time through, we gotta go at the start of the woods.

That's the 800 meters–to–go mark, and everybody's gonna be hurting." The boys nodded assent; Paul had summarized Almond's game plan. They came out of the woods and neared the final ascent, a steady hill to the finish line. "And that's it. On the first loop, we would break off here and go up the first hill again."

"I don't see why this course is so slow" Mike commented. "There aren't that many hills or turns." Paul did not know either. But he had run here seven times before, and his times were always slow. Boardman was a mystery.

The team finished running and circled around Naylor, the alternate, who led them through a routine of stretches. Naylor had developed into the team's leader – customary because he was a senior, but unusual because he was not the fastest on the varsity team. His position of authority would once have clashed with his personality; in his first three years on the team he had been the wildest, the most irreverent. But he was now the mellow senior who had invested himself totally in his team and the people on it. It hurt him not to be among the top seven, not to compete at Regionals. He had worked and improved all year, but he had started his training late and in poor shape. All of his persistence couldn't help him catch the younger runners, and he'd become an alternate after three years of varsity. He hid his disappointment well, and the friendships he'd made on the team made it rankle less. Naylor cared about his teammates, and he was happy that they had a chance to run at State even if he could not. This compassion was his greatest asset as team leader; he was first to encourage his friends.

With each different stretch, Naylor led counting. He said, "Count," and the entire team said, "*One*." "Count." "*Two*." "Count." "*Three*." And so on until after nine, when Jason instead asked, "Where're we goin'?" The reply was "State."

Almond had taught them to end every stretch by saying "State" rather than "Ten," though "Where're we goin'?" in place of "Count" had been Paul's innovation. Both deviations

       Chapter 2- The Rivals

from the pattern served to condition the Salem runners. They were like soldiers in training, repeating the word "kill" until it had no connotations. Almond's conditioning brought the State tournament into the realm of possibility, of familiarity. The circumstances were less ghastly and the consequences less real than those of war, but Almond and his runners considered themselves fighters. Paul's tweak had added an affirmation to the call–and–response. Every time they said it, which they'd done twenty times a day, five days a week, for the past two months, the Quakers promised themselves that on the day of Regionals they would prove themselves worthy of a state berth. Today they would find out if they had been speaking the truth.

The Quakers jogged back to the tent, the morose girls having vacated it.

The boys put on their spikes and the shirts of their uniforms. Then they put other shirts back over these. This was another routine they'd learned from Almond. Their uniform shirts, he'd told them, were special. Not until they reached the starting line were they to display their uniforms, like Clark Kent shedding his shirt and tie. This was a small ritual, but Salem's success had been built on the attitude nurtured by it and similar habits. "Attitude," Almond always told his runners, "is our magic."

Paul jogged to the line with the rest of his team, and he stripped off his shirt and shorts to reveal the Salem uniform. Red stripes ran down along the sides of the black jersey and shorts. Gray trim marked the uniform's edges, and silver letters spelled SALEM across the chest. In nearly any other circumstance, Paul would feel self–conscious in his skimpy outfit. But at a race, jersey number 121 was exactly what he wanted to wear. Those jerseys had attitude.

Joe's attitude felt something less than magical. Somehow this meet did not seem like the focal point of his season, or even his day. Part of him was not at all ready to run. The other part was terrified at the first part's apathy. *Wake up!* Joe shouted to himself. *It's Regionals!*

The Quakers took several striders, bursts of speed covering the first fifty yards of the course. After one of these striders they stayed out on the course rather than jogging back to the line, and they each knelt down on one knee. Almond joined them, and offered them his final encouragements.

"Guys, we're better than any team out here. Let's not just qualify. Let's beat Edgewood." He said a few other things, words to bolster their confidence and stir their spirits. Then, "Let's get a break." He put his fist in the center of their circle, and all the boys put one of theirs atop it. "S.C.C. on three," he said, quickly and without thinking. This was how they'd begun races, ended practices, and concluded team meetings throughout the year. The Salem Cross Country runners had said the familiar chant dozens of times, and they associated it with all of their successes and failures. "One, two, three," Almond started. Then everyone, shouting so that the other teams could hear: "S.C.C!"

Almond trotted away and the team gathered back together for a prayer. Yanek spoke aloud as the rest of the runners supplicated for speed and determination. "Lord, thank you for this beautiful day, for bringing us all here together. Lord, help us to do our best, and to qualify for State. Lord, be our wings and the wind beneath them. In your Son's name we pray, Amen." A chorus of amens answered him, and the Quakers were finished preparing. Now all that separated them from the race was a puff of smoke from a pistol.

They ran another strider or two to kill time and keep their muscles warm. Then the official screeched his whistle, and all of the runners – experienced enough to recognize the signal to return to the starting line – formed rows in the areas that had been spray painted in the grass for their teams. These boxes were wide enough for three of a team's runners to stand side–by–side; the rest fell in behind. Paul, Aiman, and Patrick stood first for Salem. The next row was Mike, Yanek, and Joe, with

Ryan behind them. They stood uncomfortably closely, but the proximity would last for only a few seconds. They exchanged their last "good lucks," and Paul reminded Mike of their strategy.

"Just start right beside me," Paul said, "and you'll run the best race of your life."

Joe almost interrupted. Almond's advice all week had been not to try any new race plans. But he decided not to interfere; Paul and Mike knew what they were doing. Joe's job was to focus on his own race, so he just slapped his teammates' hands and bent forward in anticipation of the start.

As the gun went off, Paul restrained himself from sprinting and immediately settled into his pace. Shortly thereafter he was nearly dead last in the Region and had his work cut out for him. At the top of the initial hill, he jockeyed to the outside of the endless pack and began moving up. Mike failed to follow him, as he was severely boxed in by the enormous group of middle pack runners. Aiman and Patrick had managed to reach the top 30 early and maintained their position around the baseball field and across the thousand–meter mark just before the course's steepest hill. As the field moved its way up the hill and then down the long gradual descent surrounded by fans towards the one–mile mark, Paul moved up into the top fifty and was in position to break into the Regional Qualifiers. He opened his first mile under 5:20, but was still barely in the top third of the runners.

Meanwhile, Joe's race was shaping up to be worse than the one two weeks ago – the one that had nearly cost him his varsity spot. He did not know how it had happened, but he had not retained any of the enthusiasm associated with qualifying for State. He finished his first mile in six minutes – on pace for the time he usually ran, but slower than he usually started. If he wanted to run as well as he had last week, he would have to run with negative mile splits. That meant increasing his pace so that the second and third miles were each faster than his first. Paul was the only one on the team who ran evenly paced mile splits, let alone successively faster ones. Joe had certainly never done this, and he knew he would not on this hot day with this ho–hum mentality. He let his feelings dictate his pace, and he slowed as he tired.

But then he ran past Naylor, who was standing along the course with a crowd of other teams' fans. Naylor shouted to Joe that he needed to pass as many people as he could, that every place was valuable. This was no revelation to either of them, as they had both heard such motivation all year. But that Naylor would say it now meant much to Joe. The senior had seen everyone ahead of Joe go by, and he had apparently concluded that the Quakers were struggling. If Salem was indeed on the cusp of qualifying, their season might come down to a tie that Joe would break. Even if the team was okay without him, Naylor's words awoke Joe's intensity. If Naylor were running he would excel under the pressure; he had always come through when the team had needed his help. He deserved that his replacement, Joe, do the same. Moreover, Joe knew that if he raced badly and the team made it to State anyway, Almond could still take Naylor in his stead. Joe shook off his inertia and began to pass runners in front of him.

The runners strung out across the starting line and broke into the woods. At this point Paul made an attempt to pass and move up into the top 25, but just couldn't find the energy to do so. By the end of the woods, and nearing the halfway point, Paul felt uninterested. He couldn't seem to go faster even though he wasn't breathing too hard and his muscles felt comfortable. It wasn't a mental block; this was the Regional meet, for which he had prepared all year. All he could do was maintain the slow pace he had been running, and despite the undemanding tempo, he caught his teammates Aiman and Patrick. The three of them all seemed lethargic, and couldn't break into the top twenty–five. They went through the two mile marker at around 11:20 and failed to make up ground on the top twenty–four. Down the straightaway again, Paul heard his dad yell out "28th" and another parent call "30th". He was close to where he needed to be, regardless of how poorly he was running. He approached the thousand–meter–to–go–mark, where he had made his move at Districts. He tried to stride out, get on his toes, do anything to move faster, but nothing was working.

Gorby and Paul broke away from the fading Aiman, and Paul took the lead in the woods. Paul thought he would again finish first on his team, until Patrick bolted past him in a sprint to the finish. At this point Paul had no idea what place he was in and didn't seem to care if he qualified individually or not. In reality, he was about 27th place, and as he made his way down to the final turn a runner fell down the hill. Paul started his kick up the grueling hill to the finish line only to see Patrick finish 23rd. There was another fallen runner, who was crawling towards the line as Paul made his way up to the finish. The runner crossed just before Paul did, making Paul the first runner not to qualify individually for the State meet. Paul quickly learned of his bad luck when he was handed a popsicle stick with a 25 written on it. He allowed it to fade to the recesses of his mind and began worrying about his team since he no longer had a chance of qualifying individually. What saved him from tearing himself apart about the race was the fact that he had beaten Aiman and come so close to beating Gorby for a second week in a row. Even if it had been a terrible race, he knew he had done well enough, comparatively speaking.

As Yanek labored towards the finish almost a minute after Aiman had crossed the line, Mooney's fifth runner blew by him in an incredible kick. Almond had incessantly stressed that every second, every point, and every runner counted, especially when it was a Mooney runner. Shortly after Mike crossed among a crowd of runners and stumbled through the chute to meet his teammates.

Joe was a chronically late kicker; he would always wait until the last two hundred yards to sprint. Today he began building up for the finish with nearly a mile to go, where Almond had told them to start turning it on. There was nothing after today for which Joe needed to save his energy: if the Quakers missed qualifying for State, their season would be over; if they qualified they would meet their goal and travel to state with nothing to lose. Joe had passed Ryan nearly a mile ago, so he no longer feared losing his varsity position. But the impetus of qualifying for State drove him forward. His capacity for abstract thinking was fading, but he congratulated himself for turning around what had been a terrible race. Joe was still battling his negative mentality: as he entered the woods for the last time he lamented that the race hadn't ended yet. But he nevertheless increased his speed; he remembered Almond saying that the woods were the place to do so. Joe zipped by nearly ten kids, any of whom might be the sixth man, the tie–breaker, for his respective team. Salem's sixth man would not allow these wild cards to best him; the sophomore pushed himself along as fast as he could.

Then near the end of the woods, with two hundred yards to go, Joe slowed. This surprised him, because he was running harder. Now was the time to expend everything he could. But his legs were not listening very well, they were barely lifting off the ground. Joe noted that everyone he had passed entering the woods was now passing him. This irked him, but he could do nothing to go faster. *I'm trying,* he told himself. He continued pumping his arms as he started up the hill that led to the finish line.

Now there was less than a football field to run, barely a basketball court. He had run over three miles today, what was fifty more yards? Joe was not thinking in these terms, and his thighs were not, either. They betrayed him and gave way, and Joe realized that he was falling. He didn't feel himself hit the ground; his endorphins dulled that shock. He did recognize that he had blown it, that he had allowed more than twenty opponents to overtake him in these last few hundred meters. He got up and struggled to keep his balance, and then staggered toward the finish. After the line his will disappeared, the conflict within him having resolved itself. His desire to run hard had been fulfilled (or, if not, there was nothing he could change now) and his urge to give up and lie down took hold. An official pulled him to his feet a few seconds later, as Ryan Griffith crossed the line.

Immediately after the race all seven runners quietly dispersed to different places. Almond was nowhere to be found; the team assumed that he fled to be alone since he was so nervous. Most of the team wandered back to the tent to mope about their races and start the what–ifs.

Joe let his parents help him back to the tent. His father's face was drawn in concern during the walk down the hill. Joseph Anthony Shivers had grown up in Salem, attended college, joined the Peace Corps, attained three graduate degrees (including a doctorate of education), taught in schools throughout the northern United States, and ultimately returned to the small Ohio town with his children and wife.

Madeline Patton Shivers, like her husband, had spent much of her childhood in Salem. The couple lived there now largely for family reasons: Joe's three living grandparents, a dozen aunts and uncles, and nearly a score of cousins all lived in the city. Joseph and Madeline thought it important that their children be close to their Grandmas and Granddad.

"Are you all right?" Mark Shivers, Joseph's youngest brother, asked as he approached. There were other benefits of living among a large, successful family. Mark was a physician – a family practitioner who was constantly attending to his own nieces and nephews.

"I feel kinda tired," Joe replied. He had by now given up all effort at anything. Joe could have tried to walk back to the tent on his own, and he could have forced himself to ignore his nausea. But the race was over, and he had done his best despite an initially poor attitude. He had run to the point of collapse; he did not feel as though he needed to be brave. On top of that, he did feel "kinda tired."

Joe's supporters set him down outside the tent, and the runner faced the ground as they discussed what to do next.

"I think we should get him an I.V." said Mark's voice. "I'm gonna go talk to the paramedics." Joe's parents said nothing; they looked almost as pale as their son. Joe, for his part, still felt sick. He drank some Gatorade, and then tried to lie perfectly still. His queasy stomach could probably take a little motion, but why risk it?

While Joe recovered, Matt and Paul managed to find each other in a set of stands overlooking the finish line. The two opponents from the past years sat together, and talked about their chances of qualifying. They talked now as teammates. The conversation shifted to prayer, whether it was out loud or feverishly in their heads. Occasionally one of them would let slip a cuss word out of sheer frustration, followed by another quick prayer to make up for it. The anxiety played with their emotions, which ranged from laughter to the verge of tears and back. As they watched other races finish, they wondered what they could have done differently, how they could have raced closer to their potential. Each second seemed to last twice as long as the previous one, and after thirty minutes the results still were not released. Finally the officials stepped out of the trailer that housed the computer scoring system and propped up a dry erase board.

By now all the D2 teams were gathered around the orange mesh fences guarding the officials. Salem draped their arms around each other to show some sort of unity. The official began writing something on the board, but no one could tell what exactly it was. She backed away and displayed to all on-lookers a notation that a tie for 6th had occurred. There was already a list of 1. through 5. on the board, and Salem was not among the teams listed.

Now the official took the marker to the final spot on the board. First came an S, and the Quakers went silent; could they have taken sixth with their poor races across the board? Next came the A, and Salem went wild. They didn't even care who had beaten them and by how much, they broke into celebration because they had just qualified for state. Before they had the chance to return to their tent, they noticed whom they had beaten in the tie–breaker: Cardinal Mooney. In fifth was Aurora, a sleeper all year. Minerva, another team no one thought had a chance took fourth. St. V's had a sub–par meet and finished third. In second was the dark horse, Hunting Valley University School, with a very solid performance. And as was expected, Ashtabula Edgewood won by almost 50 points. Walsh Jesuit finished 8th in the meet, and few people took note of it. Almond would later tell his runners that Walsh's number one runner had passed out from heat exhaustion. If he had finished the race, his team would likely have taken second, moving Salem into 7th and sending them home for a long off–season.

Joe was traveling (with assistance) to the port–a–jons when he saw the screaming mass of people rush down the hill. "We made it to State! We made it to State!" Tiebreaker for the second week in a row, Joe was swept into the arms of teammates, parents, and friends who were suddenly his number–one fans.

The team gathered with Almond back at the tent and he allowed them to view the official results. Apparently Patrick had finished before any other team's third scorer, and the Quakers were winning the meet after 25 runners had crossed the line. Salem took the 17th, 18th, and 24th team scoring spots, beating Edgewood's 21st, 23rd, and 25th top three. What killed Salem were their 4th and 5th runners, who finished 76th and 85th in the scoring compared to Edgewood's 30th and 32nd finishes. Still, the important thing was they were going to Scioto Downs and had an opportunity to redeem themselves in front of the entire state of Ohio. They could nitpick the results all they wanted after the season, but now was time for celebration. The eight varsity runners gathered in a huddle and cheered and cried and let out the loudest S–C–C they had all year. After that they continued their celebration with a victory lap around the course to let everyone know that Salem was going to the promised land.

"Isn't this the greatest feeling in the world?" Almond rhetorically asked his band of State qualifiers. They did not need to answer with words: their wide grins and war whoops sufficed. Everything they'd done to prepare for Regionals had been worth the time and energy. Even with their worst race of the year they had made the cut. They were going to State, the utopia.

The boys had planned to drench Almond with ice from a barrel–like cooler when they'd qualified, and they'd told Almond as much. Now they bore down on him, five or six against one. But their coach wove through them and escaped dry. From far off he looked like a gazelle evading the boys. Then Lance Murphy joined the chase. Lance, a junior, had joined the team this year. In track he ran the 400 and 800 meter races, but his mid–distance–runner's build had not helped him much over three–odd miles. He had been junior varsity for most of the year, running cross country to stay in shape for track in the spring. Now Lance hunted Almond, displaying a sprint that could not be extended over five kilometers. The lithe Almond was still a gazelle, but his muscular pursuer was a lion. Lance lunged and the chase was over; he held onto his coach while the other boys drenched him. Soaking, Almond peeled off his shirt and spread his lips into a wide white grin. Water ran down his dark skin, onto the thin blue pants he wore. He didn't like losing any kind of foot race, but Lance's victory over him was meaningless compared to that won by his team.

When they had wrung enough joy from the Boardman grounds, the Quakers returned to their bus. The boys sat down, as comfortable as they could remember being. The girls, happy for them but reeling from their own race, offered weak smiles. Suddenly Russ Hopple bounded aboard. Hopple was Almond's other assistant coach. He did the legwork, recording times and places throughout races, measuring training runs with his car, and otherwise helping wherever he could. He was stocky for a runner, and his career hadn't been as successful as Almond's, but he had still run in college. He now turned nervously to Joe.

"When you fell, did anyone help you up?"

The question puzzled Joe, and Hopple's manner alarmed him. He tried to recall…

"Yeah, a girl helped me up. But it was after I'd crossed the line."

"Okay, thanks." Hopple hustled away, on an errand the kids could not guess. They resumed their rejoicing.

Several minutes later Hopple came back, and Almond with him.

"Guys," began Almond, his smile nowhere. He got the attention of the runners. "Mooney filed an appeal." Teams were allowed to challenge a race's official results within ten minutes of their posting. "They said Joe should be disqualified because he got helped up." Oh no. Now they might not make it to State – but wait, Joe hadn't received any illegal aid–"And they lost!" cheered Almond. His smile swept back over his face, and relief returned to the bus. Now that the runners thought about the seemingly close call, they realized that it would not have mattered if Joe had been disqualified. Ryan, who would have become Salem's tiebreaker, had again beaten Mooney's sixth man. Salem seemed to have insurance against all eventualities.

The Quakers exchanged music and stories of their own races. The Gorbys, Patrick's parents, had scheduled a party at their house. Of course the runners could not stay up too late or eat anything too unhealthy. They were at the pinnacle of their season, headed for what was now the monumental meet of their lives: State. But the restrictions in diet and lifestyle were minor compared to the thrill of competing in Columbus. Paul summed up the team's attitude: "Pop will taste better after next week than it would have today."

After returning home on the bus, Paul, Mike and Aiman jumped into Matt's car and the three of them left to get a bite to eat. "We've got to stop at my grandma's before we get Chinese, is that all right?" asked Matt. Of course it was fine with his friends, but he always had to reassure himself by checking with them.

"We're going to State!" Paul yelled out the window, completely ignoring Matt's question. Matt's cell phone went off in the front middle seat of the car, and Matt ordered Paul to quiet down.

"Dude, shut up, my mom is calling." He answered the call and had a short conversation, then turned to his teammates. His face revealed that he had bad news to share. But Matt was known to be melodramatic, to blow things out of proportion, so the three passengers looked at each other with grins, ready to laugh at Matt's priceless expression.

"My mom just told me that there are posts on JJHuddle saying that the results have been changed and Mooney moved ahead of us by 2 points." JJhuddle was Ohio's sports internet forum. One could find updates every minute if there was a controversial situation going on. But oftentimes the posts were nothing more than rumors and hearsay.

"Those people on JJHuddle are just jealous that we spanked them today in the meet," said Aiman, showing his cocky side.

"Yeah, let's go get some food. I only had an apple and some energy bars all day," mentioned Paul. Satisfying their appetites was more important than considering empty rumors from some website.

Chapter 3

●

The Rollercoaster

*"Forsan et haec olim meminisse iuvabit –
Perhaps someday we will look back upon these
things with joy"*

– Vergil

The problems started well before the meet actually took place, when the meet officials were planning the race. They decided to go out of their way to prevent any scoring errors by introducing four backup scoring systems. As melodramatic as it sounds, this meets – like postseason events in all sports – had to run perfectly or else the officials would face backlash from very angry coaches and their bosses at the Ohio High School Athletic Association. With new technologies available, they spared no expense in making the Boardman Regional the place to be for accurate results.

Originally, before technology became more prevalent in the sport, runners pinned numbers to their chests or hips. As they finished, they would rip off a small piece of paper designating their name, team, and race number. Officials would collect the tags and place them in order through a string. This system worked flawlessly in smaller races when finishers were three seconds apart at the closest. But at the Boardman Regional, five runners might cross the line at the same time, forcing officials to determine the order they had finished. In a race as important as the Regionals, the officials' judgments were not considered accurate enough to make such decisions. The meet director needed something that worked 100% of the time: an automatic system utilizing computers and small chips placed on runners' shoe–strings.

The equipment had been available in the past, but was very expensive. Each chip cost about one dollar to rent, which adds up when there are over a thousand runners: girls and boys in all three divisions. The meet director bought into the idea since the system's record for accuracy was unblemished. The chips would score the race perfectly, and all the officials would need to do was hand out the results in the end. Each chip was individually programmed with a runner's team, name, and number, much like the tags used in the past. As a runner crossed the finish line, a detector would read the chip and add that runner to the results. After every runner had finished, a computer connected to the detector would compile all the results and print copies for all the coaches. The system seemed error–proof, but the meet director still was not satisfied.

Although rare, small problems could occur with the chips. For instance, if a runner crossed the line with his chip–less foot, and another runner behind him crosses the line with the foot that did have a chip on it, the computer would see the second runner as the winner, even though the first runner had clearly finished first. Also, if a runner lost the shoe with the chip attached to it, he or she would not appear in the results. To avoid such errors, the meet director decided to supply each runner with two chips, one for each shoe. Racers would no longer have to run back for a lost shoe or focus on with which foot to finish with first.

In addition to the chips, the meet director took his preparations a step further. He added a small camera that scanned the runner's hips as they ran by so that the officials could review the tape, look at the hip numbers, and score the race. By now, the director had gone overboard in attempting to make the race as accurate as possible, but he did not stop there. He hired a cameraman to face the finish line and use a home movie camera to tape the race head on. And finally, he brought back the tear–away tags as a last resort, just in case everything else failed.

Immediately after the boys' Division II race, the only complaint was minor–and hardly unusual. In a race with stakes as high as those at Regionals, post–race appeals are commonplace. Today the coach of Fairview, one of the several teams with a runner who had fallen near the finish line, brought a complaint to the officials. After the coach had submitted a request in writing (per OHSAA regulations), the referee and his assistants ruled on the appeal. This process delayed the release of the results, and Almond assumed that the appeal related to Salem's and Mooney's tie. In fact, Cardinal Mooney never filed an appeal.

The referee officially established the results as accurate, copies of the scoring were made for coaches to take home, and the awards ceremony began. Colin Durina of Mooney, who had indisputably finished fourth place in the race, walked with his coach to the awards table to pick up his Ohio–shaped medal. When he arrived, the official stationed there asked for his name, then handed him a fifth place medal and congratulated him. His coach, already emotional from missing a state berth on a tie–breaker, told the official that Colin had finished fourth in the race and that he deserved the fourth place medal. The official showed the coach the results, which clearly established Colin as fifth and not fourth. The coach reviewed the results in disbelief. Instead of Colin showing up in the 4th spot, a runner from Beachwood was there. Beachwood was in Mooney's and Salem's District, and had barely qualified for the Regional Meet. Their top runner had finished 20th overall, so it was extremely unlikely that another one of their runners had finished fourth. Upon further investigation, it was discovered that he had, in fact, finished dead last. The director's attempt to use technology to prevent problems and scoring errors had caused greater ones.

Meanwhile, a Streetsboro runner noticed that he did not appear in the results. He and his coach were confident he was in the top 20, but when they looked in the results his name was nowhere to be found. The Streetsboro coach informed the meet director at the same time as the Mooney coach and a coach from Pepper Pike, whose top runner had been awarded eighth instead of ninth. Now that three very important errors had been found among just the first twenty runners, the officials began to wonder if more were to be found throughout the crowded results. The awards ceremony was postponed until the race could be reviewed. Even if the 24 State qualifiers had all been accurately determined after review, the team scores might change, thus affecting the six teams that had qualified for the State Meet.

At first it seemed that since Colin Durina had moved up one spot in the scoring, Cardinal Mooney would gain a one–point edge over Salem and break the tie. However, that Beachwood runner was removed in front of every Salem and Mooney runner, so each of them moved up one point, and the scores remained deadlocked. But when the Streetsboro runner was added to the results behind Colin and in front of every other Salem and Mooney runner, Cardinal Mooney ended up with one point fewer than Salem's total. The Streetsboro runner pushed all five scoring Salem runners back a single point, but displaced only four of the Mooney runners. The officials had quite a problem on their hands, and most of the coaches had already left. To be fair to every team, coach, and individual, they decided to review the race, piece by piece, runner by runner, with their complicated back–up systems, and do the best they could to provide accurate results to everyone that had competed in the Regional Meet. However, their actions would affect two teams, both believing they deserved to represent the Region at the State meet the following week: Salem and Mooney.

By this time the Salem bus had left, and only one representative from the team was still at Boardman High School. Assistant Coach Rick Wilson had begun working for the team in 2002, when Almond was first hired. Like Almond, he had run for Malone College, like Almond, he had won All–American honors multiple times, and now he trained daily with the head coach. Wilson paced the boys during some workouts and encouraged them during races, but otherwise kept a low profile. He did not want to take away from any of Almond's status, and the two coaches' philosophies differed on virtually every aspect of running. Wilson advocated running as hard as possible for as long as possible in races, training twice a day, and avoiding all refined sugar. Almond, by comparison, seemed soft–he encouraged gradual pacing, discouraged two–a–days, and allowed the boys and girls to eat whatever they wanted on Saturdays after races. Nevertheless Almond respected Wilson, his elder by fifteen years, and he especially valued his colleague's speaking ability. When Wilson orated, he grabbed people's attention. Today, however, he said little. He just watched as the events unfolded, and he worried.

"I don't really want Chinese anymore; I lost my appetite," said Paul shortly after arriving at the buffet. "I'll just get some food at Dunkin' Donuts across the street."

"Okay, but they won't let us share food with you; they are pretty strict," replied Matt.

Paul came back to the buffet with a box of donut holes and sat down with Matt and Aiman. "Are you guys going to Gorby's tonight?" asked Matt. The answer was obvious; the team would meet for a celebration of the boy's qualification for the State Meet.

"Yeah, but I got a bad feeling about this rumor. I have terrible luck when it comes to things like this," Paul said, fairly confident that the situation had gone awry. He was used to finishing one spot short of a medal or trophy, or, in today's case, finishing one spot out of qualifying for State individually. But he used the setbacks for motivation and tried to focus more on his team's success.

"Well let's get out of here and find out what's going on with JJHuddle," Matt said as he finished up his last bite of General Tso's chicken.

Joe had gone straight home with his family after the meet. His father, the Salem Schools' Curriculum director, wanted to relish Salem's victory fully, so he had begun reading the commentary on JJHuddle. Joe's dad had been browsing the website when the first post about the scoring change appeared, and he had been quick to dismiss it. "This guy doesn't know what he's talking about," he had decided.

Joe, whose past two hours had been his happiest in months, had assumed the worst. *Looks like those two hours are all I'm gonna get,* he had reflected. He and his father had watched the posts stream in. Both had worried and wondered if everyone else on the team was seeing this. Joe's dad called his brother and alerted him to the developments.

Paul rushed into his house. His father had already heard the news from Joe's father, and by now he too had checked what the fuss was on JJHuddle. Despite knowing to some extent what was being said on "the Huddle," Paul was in complete disbelief when he read through the post. It stated that due to the removal of the fourth runner, Cardinal Mooney would move up ahead of Salem, and the tie would no longer exist. That was followed by several congratulatory comments by other runners intended for the Cardinal Mooney team. What they did not realize was that Salem had been bumped up the same amount of points as Mooney and the score remained tied. The posts seemed ignorant, nothing but poorly–educated guesses as to how the results would change. But the existence of any controversy convinced the pessimistic Paul that Salem was no longer going to the State meet.

Word traveled quickly among the team members by instant messages and cell phones; Gorby's party was bound to be full of depressed and somewhat angry runners who had already been through enough emotional stress for one day. Paul stopped on his way to his teammate's house to grab some Cherry Coke, a beverage he had not allowed himself the luxury of drinking for five months, and something for which he had desperately longed. It was a means of closure for him, a white flag raised to symbolize his giving up on the season for which he had worked so hard, only for it to end a week early. He did not want to train, to go through the stresses of running anymore. He just wanted to drink his cola and to mope with the team that had become so close.

The Gorbys lived in a two–story house on a dead–end street that saw little traffic besides kids on bikes. They, like many of their neighbors, were a middle–class nuclear family. Hal held a management job at a local manufacturing company and Rhonda, who had stayed at home to raise Patrick and his older brother A.J., was now working part–time in the school cafeterias. A.J. was in college, so Patrick was the only child left at home. Hal and Rhonda could see that Patrick loved his sport, and anyone could tell that he excelled at it. Their son had found an ideal activity; they took to their role as parents of a runner. Both were members of the X–tra Mile Club. At home meets Hal rode his ATV ahead of each race, leading the runners through Memorial Park. The Gorbys had undertaken tonight's party with enthusiasm and with sincere happiness for Patrick and his friends.

The news of the revised standings, however, had dampened the boys' and girls' moods. The cake, emblazoned with congratulations, did not belong with these mourners. The balloons lightened no faces; the Quakers drooped like the red and black streamers. The Gorby family still had some reason to be happy: Patrick had qualified for State individually and would still be competing there. But none of his teammates would be going with him, nor (more importantly) would the team. The girls faced a similar situation, sophomore Deirdre Clary and freshman Erin Murphy had both qualified independently of their team. Mrs. Gorby struggled to accept the situation, and her disappointment displayed itself to everyone to whom she talked. She lamented that no one was having a good time: she and Hal had tried to make it nice for the kids, but now... The runners, preoccupied with their defeat, did not even consider that their sadness was ruining her party.

Paul arrived relatively late to the "party," and quickly fell apart among his teammates. They sat around a small fire, reliving the day's events, and murmuring about what the future held for their team. Even Patrick, who because of his top–24 finish would run at State whether his team did or not, was holding back tears. The entire team knew he felt the same way they did, and that he would trade anything to have them line up alongside him at Scioto Downs.

Most of the boys who had run that day attended the party, as did some of the girls. A.J. Gorby was home from college, and so was Shane Harding, the team's star from the previous year. Shane had continued following the Cross Country team, and he maintained friendships with the high schoolers. He had watched Salem's boys improve since he had left; the Quakers had won more invitational meets in the 2003 season than in all of Shane's three years on the team. The circumstance frustrated him–if only he were a year younger, he could be running on this fantastic team. He too staggered under Salem's loss–a loss which never would have occurred if he, Shane, had still been running for the Quakers.

Aiman only learned the authenticity of the controversy when he arrived at the Gorbys', and he did not handle the news quite as well as the rest of the team had. While everyone else was sitting around the campfire sharing their sorrows, he disappeared.

Within a few minutes of Aiman's departure, his teammates noticed that he had left. Paul voiced their concerns, "I hope he doesn't do anything stupid. He gets so angry at himself. Should we go look for him?" Paul stood up and moved away from the fire. Beyond his desire to help Aiman, he wanted to walk around, to go someplace, to do anything but sit here.

"No," said Mike thoughtfully, "he probably just went home. We can try to talk to him online in a little while. If he's not home in a half hour, then we can look for him."

"But what if he gets hurt or something? What if he gets in trouble?" Paul worried.

"Paul, calm down," said Mike, "he's not gonna go rob a bank. He's just gonna walk home and pout a little bit." But Paul could hardly keep himself from worrying about his teammate. Anything could happen on a day as bad as today, when he had missed State by one place, when his team had missed State by one place…He sat back down and resumed meditating on the day's failures.

The girls, who had themselves barely missed a State berth, tried to comfort the boys. They talked about the current high school gossip: who was cheating on whom and that sort of thing. The girls were dealing with their own disappointment by helping the boys overcome theirs. Or, at least they were trying.

Paul, incapable of consolation from the team, began softly sobbing in his hands. It was not an audible cry, as he was trying to hide it from his friends, but the tears and emotion showed on his face as hard as he tried to stop them. His spirits were lifted when Almond called, with relatively good news. Apparently the meet director had gathered an *ad hoc* committee to review the results, and was in the process of finalizing them. Almond promised to do his best to appeal the results, as they were not in Salem's favor.

Although Almond did not have the results in hand, he mentioned that since Paul had finished 25th, one place out of qualifying individually, there was a chance he finished in the top 24 with all the errors circulating. This provided Paul some hope, but he refused to let it brighten his spirits in the midst of his teammates. The team drifted into Patrick's den to watch a horror movie. Paul was in no mood to be scared or further emotionally shaken, so he opted to go on the internet. The movie's first few minutes established a mood too horrifying for Joe, who followed after his cousin. The Shivers' surfed through online explications of the second Matrix movie, which they had recently seen together. As they read the speculation and theories about the noble Neo and his controlling robot overlords, they came across an idea. What if they found a rule, on the OHSAA website, that the meet director had broken in the process of fixing the results? That would nullify the new results and Salem would be back on track for the State Meet.

After searching the rules section for about an hour, they came across what appeared to be exactly what they needed. The rule was 7.1: "The Referee shall decide all matters relative to the application of rules. The Referee will decide on the penalty for any reported violation of the rules and will decide the final placement of competitors when a question arises.

"The decision regarding place finishers is final unless an appeal is filed in writing with the Referee within 10 minutes after the results of a race are posted."

Paul was confident no written appeal had been filed and that the original results should have been final, even if they were flawed, based upon the OHSAA's own rules. By this time the kids watching *The Ring* in the other room were getting resltess. As some of the other runners entered the computer room, Paul showed them rule 7.1.

"Guys, look at this loophole I found," Paul said. Mike Overholser bent over and examined the computer screen. Then he started to smile.

"Paul, bring up the Regional section," Mike ordered, "I'm gonna call the meet director and ask him about this." Paul clicked a few links as he chuckled to himself at Mike's audacity. Whereas Paul had wondered how he could ever use the rule he had found, his teammate had not hesitated. Mike would go to the top.

By the time Mike had found the meet director's phone number, several more of the boys had gathered around the phone. Mike had that effect on his more mild–mannered teammates; when he acted, they watched. In this case they were also listening, because Patrick Gorby had turned on the speaker phone.

"Hello?" began Mike.

"Here we go," said Paul softly. He expected any second for Mike to begin shouting at the man on the other end of the line.

"Yeah," Mike responded to the meet director's greeting, "I have a question about the Regional Meet." He proceeded to quote from the OHSAA rule, and he explained how it applied to the present situation. *Wow*, thought Paul, *he's doing a really good job with this.* Then the meet director's voice crackled that the rule was inapplicable, and that the proper steps had been taken. Mike swore loudly into the phone, the meet director bid him goodnight, and the conversation ended.

"Maybe I could go to his house," Mike offered as his teammates stared at him. Whatever the phone call had accomplished, it could not be in Salem's favor.

Paul went home that night with a million different things running through his head, and sleep was not one of them. He stayed on his computer until about 4:00 chatting over an instant messenger and reviewing various rules on the OHSAA website. The more he read the rule, and thought about how it could be applied in their specific situation, the more hope he gained. The problem was fundamental, a problem a lot of young people face: how could Paul, a 15 year old, do anything about the situation? He finally succumbed to sleep and woke up to a dreary Sunday morning. He continued his pop binge, drinking several cans while watching the Pittsburgh Steelers game at a friend's house. He had no intention of running; it would be more beneficial to begin his mandatory two–week break before track training could begin.

School district employees were late to learn about the controversy. Coach Almond first heard about the scoring errors after the bus had returned to Salem on Saturday afternoon, when Assistant Coach Wilson called him to say that the results were still in limbo. Wilson did not know specifics, but he understood that the finish line chips were thought to have malfunctioned.

Salem Athletic Director Greg Steffey called Almond several hours later. Steffey asked the coach how his teams had fared that day. Almond told the A.D. the results he had seen, but noted that the boys' race was under review. When the coach called the meet director, he was told he would be notified when the results were finalized. Almond and Steffey waited.

During the season Almond had urged his runners not to visit JJHuddle, where boasts and predictions could ignite needless flare–ups. The coach would rather his teams speak by winning races, not by blustering online. But the forum held an allure; it allowed fans and athletes to chat and bicker anonymously at all hours. Paul and Lance both had accounts, allowing them to post on the site. So did one runner's mother, and so – some speculated – did Almond himself. Even if he did not have an account, Salem's coach could (and often did) read others' posts and follow the conversations. He now turned to the site for the breaking story of the confusion about the Regional meet. What he saw there discouraged him, and none of the area coaches he knew could give him better news. When Almond called Patrick Gorby's house that night, he had almost as little information as his runners.

The meet director called Almond at 10:30 on Saturday night to tell him that Salem had finished seventh and Mooney sixth. The director explained how he and a few other people had reviewed the scoring, and that the new results were the correct ones. Wondering how to tell his boys, Almond hung up the phone.

Chapter 3- The Rollercoaster

Steffey, the athletic director, learned about the way the results had changed. He sensed that the officials' procedures were unorthodox, and a scan of the OHSAA Cross Country Tournament regulations confirmed his instincts. Only Fairview had given the referee any written appeal within ten minutes of the results postings, though the process is explained in Rule 7.1. And no team had complied with Rule 7.2, which allows teams to further protest before a jury of appeals. A team must make this second appeal within ten minutes of the referee's ruling on its first appeal. The A.D. grew confident that Salem could fight the new results. The OHSAA officials had violated their own rule.

Almond met with Steffey on Monday, and the A.D. and the high school principal called the meet director to check the facts. The Salem administration wanted to be sure it had accurate information before going further. The meet director outlined the procedure used to determine the new results, and he offered his sympathies about the whole business. Armed with a sense of justice and an OHSAA rulebook, Salem Superintendent David Brobeck telephoned the Commissioner of the OHSAA in the hopes of remedying the situation. He did not get far. Brobeck was told that the officials' ruling, however unconventional, would stand.

Brobeck hated hearing that anything could not be fixed. He was now in his third year at the Salem school district. He had arrived with dynamic ideas and plans, and had fought what he perceived to be stagnation in the school system. His views, along with his hiring of out–of–towners like Steffey and Almond, alienated him from some town residents. But Brobeck liked action, and he considered unpopularity a risk worth taking. He was a former head track coach, and after reviewing the same video tape and Finish Lynx data as the meet director, he came away unconvinced that anyone really knew who had finished where. Although relatively new to Salem, he did not want anyone to take away his students' rights. The OHSAA Commissioner's refusal only incited his energies.

But the Commissioner had limited Brobeck's options. According to OHSAA procedure, Salem could appeal the Regional results before the OHSAA Board of Control. But the Board would not meet until after November 1st, the day of the State Meet. Even if the Board could convene in time to allow the Quakers to run at State, they had no power to overturn the Commissioner's decision. OHSAA Bylaw 8, Section 3, *Decisions by Officials*, states that as far as the Board of Control is concerned, "[t]he decisions and interpretations of the rules by officials are final." If Brobeck pursued his cause, he would not be appealing through the Ohio High School Athletic Association. He, and the Salem School District, would need to go to court.

Brobeck asked the district's lawyers to prepare a motion for a temporary restraining order against the OHSAA and its commissioner. If the school district was successful, the restraining order would force the association to allow Salem to participate in the State meet. Of course the real case, the one seeking a permanent injunction against the OHSAA, would occur after the State Meet. Then the court would decide officially whether the Salem team had a right to compete.

A temporary restraining order represents "the court's ability to grant effective, meaningful relief until a determination of the merits." To obtain a favorable ruling, the Salem schools' legal team had to address four concerns: Would the school district be likely to win an injunction based on the case's merits? Would irreparable harm occur without the restraining order? Would the restraining order harm other parties? Would the restraining order serve the public interest?

Courts generally cannot decide a dispute between a voluntary organization, like the OHSAA, and its members. An exception is made if "mistake, fraud, collusion, or arbitrariness" occurs, and this last charge was the one Salem leveled against the meet officials. Because of the nonstandard procedures adopted after the race, Salem's lawyers argued that they could win an injunction based on the case's merits: the OHSAA had broken its own rules.

The Salem High School boys cross country runners would indeed suffer irreparable harm if they were prevented from running: they would miss the only 2003 Boys' High School Cross Country State Tournament ever. While the harm was not life–threatening, nothing after November 1st could ameliorate it.

As for harm to others, no individual or team would suffer if a court issued the restraining order – Salem's presence at the State Meet would not cause anyone to run any faster or slower than he otherwise would have.

Finally, the issuance of a restraining order would serve the public interest: the interest of the public of the city of Salem. Athletic recognition brings pride to small communities like Salem. The city was the site of Ohio's first womens' rights convention, and its many museums gave it a strong culture. But in no way did these factors decrease the emphasis Salemites placed on high school athletics. Citizens and organizations such as the X–tra Mile Club, the Parks & Recreation Department, and the school district itself had sacrificed so that the cross country team could succeed. If the Quakers were stopped now, and the OHSAA was later found to be in the wrong, Salem could be given no substitute for the honor of a team competing at the State Meet.

After every race Almond distributed "Coaches Comments": overviews of individual and team performances. He also included scheduling information for the next week's meet and an occasional running quote. The Coaches Comments filled one side of an eight–and–a–half–by–eleven sheet, and Almond passed them out before Monday practices. He then read through them, explaining his opinions and suggestions. Each runner received at least one sentence of performance review, and Almond included some encouragement for the future. A typical midseason Comment fit this mold: "OK race, you didn't attack like usual, you looked tired. Focus on the training right now." The Quakers liked learning what their coach thought of their races, for good or ill. They used his input to prepare themselves for their next competition.

After this Monday most of the runners would not be having a next meet for a long time, but Almond still distributed Coaches Comments. He believed that his teams would accept criticism and advice more now than ever. Coupled with the runners' dejection, his words now would motivate them during the twelve months until they could redeem themselves.

"Hats off to Patrick, Erin, and Deirdre for qualifying for the state meet!" began the Comments. "In that aspect, it was a great day for Salem CC –it will probably also go down as one of the worst days in Salem CC…" Almond proceeded to address each of his runners in turn. He steeled Deirdre, Erin, and Patrick for the excitement of State, but he could give everyone else only long–term advice. He told them to look forward to track season, to set high goals for Cross Country next year, and to pledge to themselves that they would never again allow their seasons to end this way.

Almond also used the Comments sheets to explain the confusion about the boys race, as he understood it. He referred to two distinct scoring errors that had led to the tie between Salem and Mooney. Colin Durina, Mooney's frontrunner, had finished fourth in the race; the original results placed him fifth and gave his team one extra point. Also, a runner from Streetsboro had been omitted from the first results. When the scorers added him, at seventeenth place, they moved back everyone behind him by one place. Durina was the only runner from either Salem or Mooney to beat the Streetsboro kid; thus Salem's score rose by five and Mooney's by only four. Either error, Almond wrote, would have sealed Salem's defeat. He assured his teams that the modified results contained no mistakes. The referee, whom Almond said was constrained by no time limit, had made the new scoring official at 10:45 Saturday night.

"The fact of the matter is MOONEY BEAT US OUTRIGHT," Salem's coach wrote. "It's unreal to go through what we have – we don't deserve it – we also don't deserve to go to state – Mooney does, they beat us. Put yourselves in their shoes…"

So, the teams would not move on to State. The finality was harsh, but it was better than the limbo where Salem's boys had been. The season was over.

But now Almond proposed that the boys come to train with Patrick for the week. Everyone on the team decided to stay with him – they would run with him all week and watch his race in Columbus. Almond had also allowed junior varsity runners to continue practicing with the team during the postseason, but most of these boys came only occasionally. A notable exception was Tommy Yuhaniak.

Tommy, a ninth grader, hunched his shoulders and made himself seem even skinnier than he was. His soft voice, fair skin, and mild demeanor created an impression of frailty. But on the Cross Country course he punished his frame to faster times than seemed possible. He narrowed his eyes into a three–mile wince, clenched his jaw into a nineteen–minute snarl, and flailed his arms across his chest until the finish line. His feet turned crooked when he ran and his form was terrible, but his sloppy style made his grit more obvious. Tommy had been among the top seven for most of the year; he had stayed ahead of the twelfth–grade Naylor and the eleventh–grade Josh Matthews. Then in October, he had twisted his ankle in a ditch. He thought he could treat his injury the same way he treated all other pain in Cross Country: by ignoring it and running faster. Almond eventually convinced him to take time off, but Tommy could not recover fast enough. He ran a slow time at Sim Earich the week before Districts, and his race proved that he was too hurt to run in tournaments. Ryan, Joe, and Naylor grabbed the sixth, seventh, and eighth spots. Tommy stopped running until he could recuperate.

He still came to practice, though. To remain in the mix while resting his ankle, Tommy rode his bike along with the pack. Tommy was here on this Monday, of course, and he pedaled ahead of the Quakers as they left the high school parking lot. When the runners arrived at the track to do speed work, he stood opposite the starting line and told them their 200–meter split times. He cheered for them as they ran past him, and congratulated them when they were finished. He exemplified the ideal Almond had preached all year: Tommy cared more about the team and its success than he did about himself.

The Quakers appreciated the catharsis offered by the workout. By running they could make their frustration tangible, replacing the hollowness they felt with the burn of oxygen deprivation. They knew by their workout times that they were faster than they had shown themselves to be on Saturday – if they had had the chance, they could have placed well at State. In the absence of State, at least they could give themselves the satisfaction of sprinting.

Joe returned home tired from the run and the news about Regionals. He still entertained some "what–if" scenarios, but he knew that he could not have run much faster. After all, he had run as hard as he physically could; he could not really blame himself for what had happened. State would have been great, but Salem had missed its only chance.

Then, when Joe and his parents were sitting around the living room after dinner, Joe's father began talking about his day at the administration building. "Apparently Dr. Brobeck wants to take the Regional appeal to court."

"Oh," responded Joe. "I don't know about that."

"Why not?" his father asked. "The OHSAA broke its own rule."

Chapter 3- The Rollercoaster

Joe could not articulate his objections. Basically, they came down to wanting not to cause trouble. This fit his personality and general philosophy. He had found that if he did not bother anyone – especially authority – not many people would bother him. Of course, Joe's pacifism made it easy for kids to hassle him. Joe, who considered himself stoic, could tolerate a lot of injustice if the alternative was a fight. But he usually did not have problems with bullies, because most high schoolers reciprocated his peaceful attitude.

Also, he opposed frivolous lawsuits. This translated into a dislike for lawsuits in general, because he felt that people should be like him and endure their hardships. Joe's attitude was easy for him to maintain, because no real hardships had ever befallen him. Anyway, this appeals business did not call for legal action. The Salem cross country runners should accept their loss without complaint and console themselves by knowing that their position was just. It did not occur to him that a justice system is meaningful only when people exercise their rights.

"It just doesn't feel right," Joe finally explained.

"Hey," said his father, "you know me. I'll follow the letter of the law; I drive 55. But don't hold me to any spirit of the law. The OHSAA exists to provide rules for sports, regardless of how they impact kids. Take the West Branch game." Salem's football team had just finished an agonizing season of close losses, including a last minute defeat to their biggest rival, West Branch High School. On the last play of the game Salem had been indisputably within inches of the end zone. The referee, with a poor view of the action, had made the controversial call that Salem failed to score. Some fans on both sides of the field watching from a better angle believed that Salem's ball carrier had, in fact, made a touchdown. "If those referees watched a tape of that game," Joe's father continued, "they might decide that Salem *had* scored, and that Salem *had* won. But it would not matter, because as soon as that official blew his whistle the last time, that game was *over*.

There is nothing anyone can do to change the outcome of that game, regardless of who deserved to win. It's the same way in cross country – after that ten–minute appeal period, those results cannot be amended."

Joe was still not convinced. After the physical pain he had experienced at Regionals, he did not look forward to another race. He wanted closure. What he did not want was controversy, and this appeals business seemed to be growing into the biggest fracas of his life.

"I wasn't sure at first myself," Joe's dad tried to persuade his son, "but I compared those new and old results, and the changes are just arbitrary. I saw some of that tape Brobeck was looking at. With the way some of those runners switched around, you can't convince me one way or another which team really scored fewer points."

Joe's mother had gotten more and more troubled as the discussion wore on. "I think they should just let it drop," she warned. "I think this is just opening everyone up to a lot of problems."

Almond informed the team about the legal action at practice on Tuesday. "Guys," he addressed his runners, "I've gone over and over those two sets of results, and there are, like, forty separate changes. One kid's time might change by five seconds; another's would stay the same. If the original scoring had, say, Johnny, Billy, Steve, and Tim in that order, the new one might have Billy, Tim, Johnny, Steve. For instance, a Mooney guy placed 38th in the first results, and after the changes he moved up to 36th. Okay. But the kid in 37th stayed in 37th. It just seems completely random." So Almond had not betrayed his principles of achievement; those principles did not apply in a situation when nobody who had really won. "I don't know how the court will decide. Frankly, I think it's kind of a long shot. But I want you guys to be ready just in case. Do you have any questions?"

"How are we going to race well after being emotionally drained by this entire week, Coach?" Paul asked, knowing the question was on everyone's mind.

"Don't worry about that," Almond reassured him, "it's my job to make sure you're ready." The Quakers tried to obey him; they kept training and waited for Thursday, when Salem's lawyers would travel to the Franklin County Court of Common Pleas in Columbus.

The team waited all that day in suspense either for the P.A. system to blare out an outcome or for Almond to call an after-school meeting in his classroom. But the day wore on, and no announcement came. The boys passed by Almond's room between classes, and even at the end of the day the coach claimed to know nothing yet. But he seemed distraught and appeared to be withholding something from the team. They met at the normal time, 3:00 p.m., under the tree in the parking lot as they had all year. Almond held several envelopes in hand, and said to the team that was now fully gathered, "These are the results of the court case...we'll all open them together." Everyone anxiously tore into the envelope and gazed in disbelief at the first sentence. "Unfortunately, the judge did not render a verdict in our favor –we're not advancing." The Franklin County Court in Columbus had thrown out the case without even hearing it. Apparently, it was against the court's policy to hear cases involving a school and an organization such as the OHSAA. Otherwise, there would be numerous cases disputing results or refereeing in all sports throughout the year. Almond did not go into this much detail with his team; all that mattered was that the appeal had failed.

Paul could not decide whether to read on, or just to throw the letter back at Almond for making him wait all day to read it. Eventually he finished the note, but it offered no condolence. Almond wrote that he did not want to qualify on a technicality, and that the responsibility for the predicament fell on himself and the Salem runners. He also encouraged the team to keep their heads up and focus on track and the next season. The letter ended with "SCC lives on…be proud."

Joe felt his last hopes leave him. The day, the week, and the season were over. Paul began crying again, which was a common emotional state for that week. Matt tried to calm him, but Paul quickly shook him off, only to be lambasted by Almond for being a poor teammate. Almond explained that he had prepared two letters, and unfortunately, he had had to hand out the one no one wanted to see.

Then the team went out on the last run of the season. They jogged through the familiar park and across the streets their strides had traveled so many times during the five–month season that appeared to have finally come to a close. Reality struck Paul when they got back and he climbed into Naylor's car. He began bawling, not attempting to restrain himself. He needed to get it out of his system, and come to grips with the situation. Almond told him about how great a track season he was going to have and that his whole running career was ahead of him. But he failed to realize that Paul was a sophomore in high school, who had just been through more stress than he had experienced in his life. He rode off with Naylor, finally composing himself, and went home.

Chapter 3- The Rollercoaster

Chapter 4

The Longest Run

"Pressure is nothing more than the shadow of great opportunity."

– Michael Johnson

Paul was still teary–eyed when he arrived home and walked down to his basement to use his computer. The rollercoaster ride was finally over, and Salem would have to wait another year for the State Meet. When Paul's dad, a dentist, came home from work at 5:00, he quickly noticed that Paul was distressed over something and asked what the problem was. Paul explained the court loss, the letter, and the relief of not having to worry anymore. He could now enjoy his two weeks off and rest his tired body and mind.

Paul began sobbing again. His dad asked, "What are you crying for?" Paul restated that the team was *not* running at State – they had lost the court case. But his father seemed still not to understand.

"Pack your bags…" his dad said, "you're going to State. The administration is filing the case again in Columbiana County, and if necessary, in Mahoning County as well." The case could be tried in the home counties of both the defendant (Franklin County, which had dismissed the case) and plaintiff (Columbiana), as well as in the county where the race had occurred (Mahoning). "Members from the community chipped in to pay for your trip down and the hotel stay. If the court case is won, the school will cover it. Otherwise, at least you'll have the opportunity to cheer on Patrick and see the race you're going to win next year."

Apparently the ride was not over; Salem still had a shot at running on Saturday, and his father made it seem like there was a solid chance. Paul hastily threw his clothes and toothbrush and running gear into a suitcase, paying close attention to the essentials: his Salem jersey and spikes. As he was rushing through the house searching for various things, Almond called to break the good news. Paul tried to act surprised, but the call was merely a confirmation of what his dad had already told him. After gathering the necessities, Paul talked to a few of his teammates online. Paul brought up the idea of attending a morning mass at his church, St. Paul, the next day. Mike was not Catholic, but accepted the offer to solicit divine help by going to church. Aiman and Matt decided to join Paul and Mike the next day. Yanek was deeply involved in his own church, and Aiman often went there with Yanek when the two hung out. They all desperately wanted to go to State, and prayer could not hurt.

Paul was dropped off at Mass at around 7:45 on Friday morning, and he waited outside anxiously for his comrades. He was worried that they might disrupt the Mass or cause a problem, even though it was extremely unlikely. Eventually, he went into the church and continued waiting, but they were nowhere to be found. Finally, he went back outside and saw all three of them with their bags in hand, just standing. "How long have you guys been waiting here?" Paul asked. He led them into the church for a half hour service. Paul's mom picked them up afterwards, and they reached the high school parking lot around the end of the first period of the school day.

On paper, Joe was a smart guy. He maintained straight A's, scored well on standardized tests, and had won the city spelling bee in each of the four years he was eligible(fifth through eighth grade). Despite his intellectual gifts, however, he had a tendency to miss important details. For example, he alone of the ten Salem runners traveling to State went to school Friday morning. He entered the high school with his duffel bag over his shoulder and headed to first period Latin. Mike and Paul both took the class, but neither of them was here today. Joe began to understand that he had made some kind of mistake. Frustrated at attending school when he evidently did not need to do so, Joe sat through the class.

During Joe's second class of the day, he saw that the clock was nearing nine, when the Quakers were to meet. He asked the Health teacher to excuse him, and he hurried down to the foyer. Almond and the other runners, all of them recently arrived, stood with their own suitcases. Patrick Gorby, Paul, Aiman Scullion, Matt Yanek, Mike Overholser, Ryan Griffith, Jason Naylor, Deirdre Clary, and Erin Murphy would all be taking the three–hour trip southwest. A few of the girls who would not be running stood by the doors, sending the two girls and eight boys on their way with hugs and smiles.

The three individually qualifying Quakers showed the stress. Patrick was not pestering the older boys as he often did. His fellow freshman Erin Murphy, a usually voluble blonde, said little and stared into the distance, as if trying to see the stadium 150 miles away. Deirdre carried her burden rather differently.

Deirdre, a sophomore, led the girls' team by example. She had started running track as an eighth grader and cross country as a freshman. She quickly surpassed her more experienced teammates. The coaches disagreed about her raw ability – Almond did not think she had much talent, and Wilson thought she was a natural – but everyone around her recognized her determination. Deirdre's demeanor gave credence to Wilson's belief: that she was the complete package, that ideal blend of talent and heart. While Almond and Wilson worked out with the fastest boys, Coach Hopple paced her ahead of all the girls. She never showed worry before races, and she generally conquered her competition. Of course, Deirdre made everything look easy. She kept up her straight–A average in the same way she accepted her role as one of the prettiest girls in school: with grace and good humor.

Her behavior today contradicted her customary appearance in every way save one: she still held her ever–present thermos of coffee. She looked as though she had run a race all through the night; her brown eyes showed that she had State in her head. She sipped caffeine and chattered worries, as though the stress of the imminent race was transforming one into the other. Strangest of all was her nervousness. Deirdre could face a nuclear apocalypse with aplomb: she would just turn her focus from running and school to stockpiling non–perishable foodstuffs. But this meet was shaking her. Where was the confident girl who always wore a bright smile?

The remaining runners, the other seven boys, displayed their excitement, too. But they did not spend much time preparing for a race they might not run; the week had siphoned their emotional energy. The waves of hope and disappointment had weathered them smooth; the Quakers could accept whatever awaited them, be it a positive ruling (and a race) or a negative one (and all–night, end–of–the–season party).

In his minivan, Assistant Coach Hopple drove Patrick, Deirdre, and Erin – the runners who were certain of their places on the starting line – along with Naylor, who would almost as surely not race. The individual qualifiers, preparing for the State meet, did not need exposure to the boisterous boys. To keep the groups separate, Almond took the rest of the team in a van owned by the school district. His passengers could and would kick back on the three hour trip. They sang along to their favorite music, most of it pop and most of it obscene. The quiet Joe surprised Almond by belting out the lyrics of his brother Brian's rap CD, but the coach should not have been wondered. After a week of turmoil, Joe felt like having fun.

Paul could not wait for the trip to be over; he was not accustomed to long drives. He passed the time by phoning his mom incessantly, asking for updates on the court case. She promised to call as soon as she heard anything, but he called anyway, just in case she could not reach him for any reason.

An hour or so into the trip, Joe petitioned Almond for a bathroom break. The coach pulled into a gas station, and the boys clambered out of the van. The road trip had excited the Quakers, who were already keyed up from the week's stresses. They sought an outlet in harmless hijinks.

"Hey," laughed Yanek at the prophylactic machine that graced the wall of the gas station bathroom, "look at that. I'm gonna buy one. Do any of you guys have change for a dollar?" Paul handed him four quarters and walked into a stall as Yanek bought a neon blue condom. "Mike," urged Yanek, "you should blow it up like a balloon."

The boys each had a role in a given conversation or escapade: Mike Overholser was the one most likely to try something crazy. But even he was not game for this stunt. "I'm not putting my mouth on that thing," Mike grimaced. Yanek decided to inflate the thing himself, and the resulting sight gag was worth more than the fifty cents he had paid. The boys all giggled, and Mike flushed red with mirth.

Meanwhile, Aiman decided to play with Paul, who was in one of the restroom's two stalls. The soccer player had a knack for aggravating people, and here was an easy victim. Paul's temper flared at minor insults – when his teammates teased him about his good–looking mother, for instance. Knowing his volatility, the runners seized any opportunity to joke about her. Paul always rose to the bait. So when Aiman grabbed a dripping–wet plunger from the bathroom floor and shook it over Paul's head, he expected a fiery reaction. He was not disappointed.

Paul stormed out of the stall. "*Ai*man!" The accused danced backward, grinning at Paul. Their faces were level – both stood at six feet two inches, though Aiman's curly hair made him seem even taller. Paul saw the amusement in his teammate's eye and tried to restrain his own smile. "I'm gonna *kill* you," he threatened, knowing he would not even try. Paul set his long jaw and reared back, but shoved Aiman only hard enough for him to feel it. The two would not really fight, nor would any other pair on the team. The Quakers had been bonding since the summer, and the State debacle had drawn them even closer.

✳ ✳ ✳

The Cross Country Inn looked like what it was, a budget motel. The runners required no frills. A bed to sleep in through the night would suffice: anything more would be excessive.

Almond set off for the lobby, leaving the kids to share stories of the ride up. Then the runners, restless from the journey and anxious about the trials ahead, occupied themselves by throwing berries at each other. They yanked the fruit from the trees in the parking lot, and the skirmish stretched from the pavement to the second–story walkway. At least a dozen times someone called for a truce: "Okay, guys, let's stop. We're gonna get in trouble." Each respite lasted a few seconds before someone else got bored and pelted the pacifist with a juicy missile.

The berry fight stopped for good when Almond appeared after a few minutes and herded the kids to their rooms. The boys and girls schlepped their luggage up the stairs and into their quarters, and then they piled back into the vans. It was time to see the State Championship course. Scioto Downs functioned for most of the time as a horse–racing track, but for one day every year it held the most important cross country meet in Ohio. The Quakers knew it in its latter capacity; to them it existed only for tomorrow morning.

No one in Almond's vehicle talked as much now, and the singing was subdued. The nearer the van drew to the stadium, the more tightly the Quakers' faces drew. Feeling the tension,

Almond switched on the radio. On came the middle of a double–entendre–filled song about a Mexican Popsicle. The Quakers laughed – nervously at first, and then with less and less restraint. Singing the refrain, they disembarked into the gravel parking lot.

The runners approached Scioto Downs from behind the grandstands. As they passed under the thousands of seats, they remembered Almond saying what the stadium was like when it was full. When the boys emerged and walked onto the racetrack itself, they glanced backward at the rows and rows of empty seats. Some early fans had already put up signs for their hometown teams and runners: sheets of cloth and paper hung from the balconies and walls. Despite all of these banners, the stadium seemed empty and small. Could ten thousand cross country fans really fit in this place? Could they bring these silent grounds to life with their shouting?

The Quakers began jogging around the field in the center of the racetrack. A wall covered with ads for beer and cigarettes encircled the dusty oval, and beyond that stretched acres of grass. The State cross country course began and finished inside the stadium, before the crowd, but most of it took place outside in the fields. Almond had run here three times, and he explained the entire course as his runners jogged sections of it. There were no wooded paths and no spirit–crushing hills, just the stadium and the rolling plains around it. The Quakers knew it was one of the fastest courses in the state.

The course began and ended on the infield of the racetrack itself, and contained two loops that stretched outside the stadium. Only coaches, athletes, and the press could get onto the field; casual fans watched from the grandstands. These spectators would all be cheering for their own hometown runners, but Almond told his boys that during the race, it would sound like the entire crowd was cheering for Salem.

Other teams were out on the grounds familiarizing themselves with the course, and OHSAA officials walked around making ready for the meet. The boys sensed that everyone was watching them. They imagined what the others were saying to each other:

"There's Salem, the team that didn't qualify."

"There's Salem, the jerks who had to go to court to get here."

"There's Salem; they just couldn't accept that they lost, fair and square."

Of course no one here would say that loudly enough that the runners could hear them, and maybe no one here recognized the Quakers at all. But the past week had left the boys somewhat paranoid. The pundits on JJHuddle condemned the decision to involve lawyers, and the runners themselves still cringed when they reflected on the legal proceedings.

Almond did not seem sure that the school district was doing the right thing, either. When it had looked like the year was over, he had told his runners that they had legitimately lost and should not want to go to State on a technicality. But when State still appeared to be an option, Almond let his superiors convince him that the revised Regional results were inconclusive. State was too important to deny himself and his runners. And those new results *were* questionable; it seemed to him as though the officials had rearranged kids randomly.

As the team jogged back onto the track's grassy infield to conclude its run, Almond's phone began to ring. He quickly halted the jog and answered the call. It was Mr. Beatty, the high school principal, with the court results. Almond's face lost color as he waited for the answer, staring wide–eyed at his team. After a short conversation, he swung the cell phone away from his face, closed it, and screamed as if the hundreds of other runners and coaches were not there. "We're running!" he exclaimed to the eight boys, who began celebrating their second State Qualification in a week. They huddled up, and Paul felt that it was his turn to show leadership for the team.

"We have something to prove now," he told them. "We have to prove we belong here. Before, I would have been satisfied with just making it here, but now I want more. Let's kick some ass, and show everyone that Salem deserved to run in the State Meet."

The conference finished with a break, and Almond directed them to the starting line to find their blocks. The officials had just received word about the results as well, and created a new block for Salem adjacent to the individual runners' starting block. As he walked with the boys to the end of the starting line, Almond spotted his former high school coach, who had since taken over the girls' head coaching job at Perry. As he walked over to tell his old coach the good news, Almond instructed his boys to familiarize themselves with the territory.

The boys sat in the grass, laughing and talking about how fast they would run at the meet tomorrow. The course looked a lot nicer now that they knew they would be running on it. Matt Yanek, however, did not show the same confidence and excitement as the rest of the team. Paul noticed his dreary face and asked him, "What's wrong, Yanek?"

"I feel so drained," the upperclassman said. "I don't know if I even want to run." That puzzled Paul. He had felt the same way himself earlier in the week, but hearing the news that he could run tomorrow had reversed his mindset.

"Maybe you should talk to Almond," Paul offered. If anyone could talk Yanek out of his funk, it would be his coach.

"Yeah," said Yanek, lifting his chin a little. "Maybe I'll talk to Coach." But his eyes drooped, and Paul could tell that his teammate was still apprehensive.

Routines define athletes' preparations. Ten minutes before every race, the Quakers headed to the line and stripped to their uniforms. Forty minutes before every race, Paul swallowed a tangerine Powergel while gagging at its flavor. The night before every race, Joe left the Salem High School football game as early as the marching band director would let him.

And the evening before every race, Salem runners sat down to their pre–race dinners.

Carbohydrates defined these meals; pasta and bread served as entrees. Almond encouraged his teams to consume carbs all the time, especially the nights before races. Carbs gave energy, carbs kept alertness, carbs fueled speed. Maybe the physiological benefits of carb–loading manifested themselves more in marathoners than high school cross country runners. But noodles conferred the psychological comfort of eating what the champions did.

Dining at the Spaghetti Warehouse was a tradition for racers across the state. Salem runners had supped there before every State tournament the team had attended in the past decade, and, since his own high school days, Almond had known it as the only place to go. The Warehouse did not just supplement the State experience – it comprised an important part of it.

The Spaghetti Warehouse had been built in the shell of a real warehouse, and its décor consisted of defunct machinery and other industrial artifacts. Some of the parents who had made the trip met the runners there, giving their son's or daughter's dinner a more familiar feel. Salem's contingent got a table on the second story, away from the chaos of the first floor and the dozens of other cross country runners eating there. Spirits and appetites were high, an effect of gaining a definite answer about State. The boys and girls filled their bellies with bread and salad and pasta. And lots of water.

On their way out, Mike and Aiman snagged the salt and pepper shakers from their table. Once outside, they showed off the theft to their teammates, chuckling at their feloniousness. Joe did not understand why they would steal for no reason other than momentary amusement. He thought of himself as a "good kid," and his scrupulosity always trumped any desire for mischief. He exclaimed something stupid to the effect of: "Oh Jeez, Mike…"

Mike grinned at Joe's anxiety. Disapproval only encouraged him; he handed the shakers to Joe. Now the "good kid" faced a dilemma. Return the salt and pepper, implicating himself and his home town in theft, just so that the restaurant could throw them away as a precaution? Or abet the crime, and run tomorrow with the blot on his conscience? The boys were almost at the van; they were leaving. Joe left the salt and pepper behind a parking block. They were just two tiny pieces in the collection of an enormous restaurant. He felt like a hypocrite.

On their way back to the hotel, the Quakers stopped to shop at a Big Bear. Almond explained that the X–tra Mile Club would pay for everything they bought, just as the organization had treated them to their spaghetti dinner. They were to purchase essentials for tomorrow morning: water, Gatorade, bagels, energy bars, and fruit. The boys and girls dispersed to grab their free groceries, and met back at the checkout line twenty minutes later. They had shopped as individuals, and everyone had picked up more than enough. Bagels came in bags of six, so anyone who wanted a couple of them got four extra. Fortunately, the X–tra Mile Club was generous.

When they arrived back at the Cross Country Inn, Almond called the team, boys and girls, to his room for their last meeting of the year. The Quakers arranged themselves on the beds and the heater, and Almond and Wilson stood inside the loose circle. The coaches proceeded to profile every runner in the room, reducing their seasons to a few evaluative sentences. They praised Deirdre for her work ethic and complimented Erin and Patrick on the natural ability that they had developed. The coaches had not expected the newcomers – Aiman, Mike, and Ryan – to be so good. Joe was a completely different runner from last year. Naylor, the alternate, should be racing tomorrow but knew why he was not: he had neglected his training in June, July, and August. Paul and Matt, veterans of the sport, could have breakout performances any day. Make it tomorrow. "Why not break sixteen?" Almond asked Paul rhetorically, challenging the sophomore to improve on his best time by nearly a minute. The coaches dangled high goals in front of each of the runners. Maybe one of the Quakers would meet the expectations; maybe they all would.

Then Almond yielded the floor to the boys and girls, who were to say which of their teammates had most inspired them throughout the year. Deirdre named Erin ("not just because she's here"), and Erin ("not just because she's here") chose Deirdre. The name that the eight boys mentioned most was that of Tommy Yuhaniak, the freshman. Tommy had spent himself in every workout, Tommy had tolerated their teasing, and Tommy had attended practice every day even though he was injured and his season was over.

When everyone had spoken once, Almond encouraged them to keep talking and mention other teammates. The coach was cherishing the team he had helped to weave, and he wanted to wring the camaraderie from the runners' hearts. Kind sentiments would benefit no one if kept secret, but every motivational anecdote a kid mentioned tonight would bind the team closer tomorrow. Eventually everyone said all he or she could, and Almond dismissed the meeting with an "SCC on three." It was almost ten o'clock when he sent the runners to their rooms.

Almond had assigned roommates before learning that the school district had won its restraining order. As such, he had arranged his runners to ensure that Patrick, the sure bet, would be able to get to sleep. Ryan, Paul, and Joe – the quietest of the Salem boys – would be rooming with him. That left the more rambunctious quartet of Mike, Aiman, Yanek, and Naylor sharing quarters.

The original plan, the one anticipating a negative court ruling, had called for Paul, Ryan, and Joe to leave Patrick and play video games all night with their four teammates. When they had checked into the hotel that afternoon, the Quakers had noticed that the televisions were incompatible with any video game consoles. Paul, who had enough of a grasp of technology to see when an idea would not work, had abandoned the old agenda and proposed a more ambitious one. The runners would all chip in money to buy a TV at a Wal–Mart, use it all night, and return it the next day. The hitch in this new plan was that Salem Schools had won the case and restored the responsibility of running to the boys. Partying till dawn was cancelled. The only game Ryan, Patrick, Joe, Paul played was a quick one of blackjack.

Once the four of them had finished brushing their teeth and performing their other nightly routines, they climbed into bed to rest before their biggest race so far. Almond had taught them that "the night before the night before" the race was the sleep that mattered, but Paul still did not want to be groggy the next morning. Although he would have liked to room with Aiman and Mike and have a good time, he desperately wanted to run the race of his life the next day, so sharing a room with his quiet teammates was a good thing. At least, it would have been if those teammates were actually quiet. Paul and Joe wanted only to get to sleep, but the boys in the other bed seemed more interested in joking around all night.

Gorby would make some raspberry noises with his lips, he and Ryan would laugh, and Paul would yell at them to be stop. After a few seconds of silence, the noises and the suppressed laughter would resume, and the cycle would begin again. Even Joe, whose teammates usually respected him, could not get them to relax. Eventually, the two cousins fell asleep despite the annoyances. Certainly, Paul thought just before he dozed off, the other, supposedly rowdy room was sleeping by now.

Paul and Joe woke up at 7:30 the next morning to more noises by Ryan and Patrick. Like so many adolescent males, they found perpetual amusement in farting sounds. Like so many adolescent males, Paul stayed in bed for as long as he could, demanding that the other bed be quiet. He finally surrendered after several futile threats and got dressed for the meet. He began packing his bags, as the team would check out of the hotel before traveling to Scioto Downs. He always feared leaving something valuable behind, something that he would need for the meet, so he double–checked under the bed and in the drawers of the TV cabinet. When he was satisfied with his search, Paul walked over to Aiman's room to wake the others up.

He was greeted at the door by Mike, who quickly filled Paul in on his night and morning. "Dude, there's this girls' cross country team in our hotel, in a room across the parking lot. We snuck out last night and went over there until, like, 3 AM." Paul shook his head and said nothing. Did they have no concept of delayed gratification? "But none of them were very good–looking," Mike continued, smiling at Paul's disapproval. "This one girl had a huge knot on her forehead, and we were laughing at it the whole time."

"Hey," said Yanek from inside the room, "that's 'knot' funny!" He walked to the door and greeted Paul. "Did Mike tell you about when he tried to touch me last night in bed?"

"That's a lie!" retorted Mike, as Yanek started laughing. "That never happened!" Aiman and Naylor approached the other boys, and they hooted at Mike's denials. The imaginary incident would be the center of conversation for most of the morning, and it gave the runners some comic relief at Mike's expense. They were still retelling the story as they stepped off the van into the parking lot of Scioto Downs.

Joe calculated that he had drunk a gallon–and–a–half of water since waking up. He would not be dehydrated during this race, he could be sure of that. But his precautions did not ease his mind, everything was a stressor and he had a race in less than two hours.

The water gave him something to do, at least: every fifteen minutes he made for the restroom. On his way, Joe passed throngs of runners, relaxing, stretching, or celebrating depending on what time they raced. Each of them wore their bright school colors and team–issued shirts; Joe had never seen so many people with inspirational quotes on their backs. But instead of exciting him, all of the commotion daunted him. "The truth is you can always run faster," read one shirt. "Sometimes the truth hurts." Joe cowered; he did not want pain. He wanted this cross country madness – his school system's lawsuits, his teammates' antics, his own worrying–to end. Joe entered the bathroom. Clearly the proprietors of Scioto Downs did not think their clientele was the kind that cared about pristine facilities. He waded through an inch of fetid water on his way through the restroom, and when he exited, he again had to run the gauntlet of motivational clothing.

Eventually Joe tensed to the point he could hardly even think about running. *All right,* Joe thought, *if I race with this attitude I'll run even worse than I did at Regionals last week. If I relax and try to have fun, I may not set a P.R., but at least I'll run a decent time. Anyway, isn't State supposed to be fun?* He considered the accusations leveled at his team, and his own doubts. *Maybe we don't deserve to be here. Maybe I did, in effect, steal those salt and pepper shakers. And maybe I don't care what people think. I'm here to run.* He took the field with an unburdened conscience.

The Quakers jogged over to their designated starting block and began to loosen up for the race. After several striders and some quick stretching, the team met fifty yards from the line with Almond for a few last words of advice and motivation. It was nothing new to a team that had raced together all year. After a short prayer led by Yanek, they trotted back to the line in preparation for the race. Paul jogged over to Aiman, and put his hands up for a high five. "All–Ohio, baby, that's all you need to think of," Paul said to him. Aiman replied with a simple nod, and headed back to the line. Neither of them realized what finishing top–25 in the meet would require. Paul had barely finished top–25 in his region, and Aiman had not broken the top 30. But to Paul the top 25 was just that, a number, something attainable. Whether it was confidence or ignorance, Paul knew that he would finish in the top 25; all he had to do was run. The starter called the racers to the line, and went through the familiar commands. As the gun went off, the sixteen teams and forty–plus individual qualifiers set out to the first turn. Mike let the effects of a last bit of nervousness dribble down his leg in his first strides, which would later become one of his favorite stories to tell.

Virtually every cross country runner opens each race with a sprint to establish position. After a few hundred meters of sprinting, he settles into his race pace, the one he will maintain until he kicks at the finish. The experienced racers at State understood this process: most of the eventual winners took the lead in the first straightaway. Accompanying the lead pack were the overeager kids who were so excited to be at State, they forgot that the race lasted three miles. These tenderfeet would fall away from the frontrunners like scrap metal from a rocket on re–entry.

Joe started near the back of the mass of bodies pushing toward the first turn. That was fine, because most of the runners here would beat him badly. Joe could accept losing to the fastest high schoolers in Division II; he deluded himself with no fantasies of individual championships. His goal was to beat every other team's sixth runner, thus ensuring Salem's victory in any tie.

To run well, Joe had decided that he must focus on two factors: his mood and his pace. Regulating his thoughts was simple enough once he had decided to have fun. *I'm running at State,* he thought, *and I'm the sixth man, so I barely matter. The world hates our team already. Why not enjoy the experience? I'll remember this day for the rest of my life; might as well make the memory happy.*

Controlling his pace was more complicated. He had decided that the mistake he had made most consistently throughout the season was slowing down too much after his opening sprint. Once a runner settles into a pace, changing it requires tremendous effort. It is simpler to establish a faster speed from the get–go. Today, Joe concentrated on this transition from sprinting to "race pace," because he was sure that his shift had been poor at Regionals. As he turned the first corner, he felt himself decelerating. In past races, Joe had willed himself to slow down at this point. Now he understood that race pace should come naturally; his body had been through enough 5Ks that it could sense the correct speed. Sure enough, he settled into the perfect pace to set a personal record.

Paul's strategy involved maintaining his opening pace; he began as fast as he ran the entire race. Wanting to get a feel for the race, he immediately dropped to the back of the field. Aiman moved ahead to hang with the front, and the rest of the team fell into their respective places. Around the first turn, the entire pack bottlenecked, slowing almost everyone to a standstill. St. V's had nearly all of its runners leading the race at this point, but Paul did not worry. They would lose their position soon enough. As the field strung out around the inside of the track on the freshly mowed course, Gorby and Paul fell into stride with each other.

"My shoe's falling off," Gorby fretted. "I didn't tie it tight enough." Paul did not reply to his teammate. It was not that he did not care, but he had no need to waste energy talking or even thinking about the problem. If the freshman's shoe (and its chip) fell off, he would have to carry it for the rest of the race; that was all. Gorby apparently reached a similar conclusion, and he fell silent. He and Paul maintained their mid–pack position for much of the first mile. They began moving up in the field only when everyone's adrenaline rush was over, and the real race began. They exited the stadium and started up a hill to the first mile. Aiman crossed first, then Gorby, and then Paul in a relatively fast time of 5:15. Despite the solid split, Paul was in 62nd place, well out of All–Ohio contention.

A few minutes later Paul could no longer see Aiman or Patrick, but he continued the steady pace that allowed him to pass the runners who had gone out too fast. He ran by a pack of Mooney runners just before re–entering the stadium, which gave him a shot of motivation to push the pace. Bursting through the hole in the stadium wall was exhilarating: thousands of fans on their feet screaming, ringing cow bells, and waving signs. Paul felt as if every person in that stadium was cheering for him. Almond had talked about the "wow" effect, and how it's tough to stay focused during one's first race at Scioto Downs. But the crowd made Paul forget about the pain and push on. Over the next half–mile loop around the track, he gained a lot of ground on the top runners and managed to pass Patrick by the 2 mile mark. The last time he had pulled ahead of the younger runner was Districts, the best race of his life. He crossed the two–mile mark in 10:52, matching his personal record from the previous spring's track season. Aiman was now in his sights, and Paul still had plenty of gas left in the tank. The field broke out of the stadium for the second time, now following the course past several horse stables and into an open field.

Two miles into a 5k, the inclination is to slow down. A runner feels his body weakening, feels the arid burn in his throat, feels the sweat soaking his skin. No one near him seems to be hurting; everyone looks as though he would be comfortable running forever. *Why even try to stay with them, when I'm feeling like this?* He is tempted to think. *I'll slow down, and then I'll feel better.*

Experienced runners know that the pain they feel is no worse than that of everyone around them, and not enough to do any real harm. Besides, why slow down now? They will feel no better; their lungs and legs will hurt just as much. The smart runner increases his effort in the last mile, intimidating his competition and finishing strong. Paul was a smart runner.

He finally caught Aiman with around 1,200 meters to go in the State Championships. Salem's top three runners were in the same position relative to each other and the competition as the week before, except this time top 25 meant All–Ohio. They rounded the lonely bend at the bottom of the left outer–loop's hill and made their way back up the rolling path. At this point, Paul took the lead from Aiman and prepared to reclaim his team leadership in front of 10,000 people. At the crest of the hill pain set in, and he eased his blistering pace. Seconds later, he was overcome by his two teammates, who were tearing by opponents in unison. Paul knew how powerful two teammates were together, and did not want them to get away from him. He was not going to be satisfied with third place on his team, because this was the State meet. That meant he needed to begin kicking now; Gorby would win a sprint if he was near Paul at the finish. He lifted his knees and dug in his spikes with 700 meters to go in the race. All he had to do was give everything he had left for a little over two minutes and he would put his team in excellent position to place well in the meet.

Just before the threshold of the stadium, Coach Wilson stood cheering for the Quakers. "Twenty–first place!" Wilson yelled out in a reedy voice. "You've got 500 meters left; kick it in!" Paul's incredible last mile had put him in All–Ohio contention. When he finally re–entered the stadium, the course ahead looked almost empty. Again the crowd made him forget the pain, the stress – everything but the finish line.

As Paul crossed the horse track, he saw Almond standing on the cinders. "You're in twenty–second," Salem's coach shouted as Paul crossed the horse track. "Go, Paul!" He turned onto the grass near the final stretch. He was still kicking as hard as he could, but now everyone around him was also starting to sprint. Suddenly a runner passed Paul, and then another; he lost track of his place but continued the brutal pace. Around the last bend, Paul saw the finish line and the clock, which read in the mid–16's. A possible personal record added to his motivation as he drove towards the finish.

Then absolute terror swept over Paul. His legs turned to jello, his arms went numb, and he simply could not lift his legs anymore. Like Joe at Regionals, Paul reached his body's limits. As he would later see on video, it looked as though he had run into a proverbial brick wall. Just then, Patrick flew by him and crossed the line mere seconds ahead of him. Paul finished in a time of 16:52, but did not yet know if he had done well enough to be considered an All–Ohioan. Aiman, whose kick was not strong, dropped back in the last stretch and finished in a time of 17:03. He was still unable to break the 17 minute mark, despite a solid performance.

Mike bore into the home stretch with three strong miles of racing behind him. His time, 17:44, was nearly the same as two weeks before, at Districts, and well faster than his Regionals race. The only flaw came in the last two hundred meters, when Cardinal Mooney's fifth runner sprinted by him. If the Salem team had any true goal, it was to prove that they deserved to run at the State meet, and the best way to do so would be to beat their private school rival. Somehow Mike let the runner by him. Otherwise Overholser had thrived under the pressure at this, the biggest meet of his short career. He had placed 96th overall and 52nd among scorers, enough to put the Quakers in contention for a good team finish. He had filled the fourth spot nearly as well as Yanek ever had; the race was probably the best he had ever run. Nevertheless, the Salem sophomore would spend the next twelve months wishing that his finishing sprint had been three seconds faster.

Yanek wheezed his way across the line over half a minute later, in 18:15. He complained of asthma; his breath was short and his face was pained. Of course, those same symptoms would appear whether the junior had suffered an asthma attack or simply choked under State's high stakes. The way Almond yelled at him suggested that the coach was betting on the latter affliction. But nothing could change Yanek's finish now. Salem's five scorers were in; all that remained was for the results to be calculated.

Meanwhile, Joe finished off a mediocre race with a fantastic sprint. He had left too little on the course, had let himself relax too much. 18:41 was a slow time for a sixth man –

Edgewood's had run 17:15. Maybe his strategy of controlled apathy had kept him from choking, but it definitely needed refining.

Ryan Griffith ran his race with the opposite problem. Accustomed to having fun with the sport and running instinctively, the cherub–faced sophomore had let the big meet psych him out. His final time of 19:01 disappointed him, but he had not come to Columbus to run a personal record. He, like the other Quakers, hoped above all that the team had done well.

When the entire team had finished, they met with Almond behind the officials' trailer. Almond was nervous as ever, and it appeared in the way he spoke, walked, and even breathed. "Our top three guys ran an amazing race," Almond summarized, "so I know we've got a solid chance of placing well." Paul gave high–fives to Gorby and Aiman. "But our fourth and fifth guys are gonna hurt us." Mike Overholser bit his lip, and Yanek, still wheezing, stared at the ground. Almond usually tried not to assign individual responsibility for the team's performance, but at State the bottom line was the outcome.

"Edgewood definitely won," the coach continued. "They had five guys in the top forty of the race. But after that there were a ton of good teams, mostly from our Region. Mooney finished pretty well. Their best guy, Durina, took fifth overall." Paul lost focus on his coach's assessments. He knew he had given his team everything he had. Even though he had failed to beat Patrick in the last race of the season, he was satisfied with his time, his place, and – most importantly – his effort for the team. He sat on a pile of pebbles and waited for the results to come in.

Fifteen minutes passed. A reporter noticed the results posted on a pole and called to Almond. Almond ran over to check them. The boys stood up to watch his reaction. The coach peered down among the small crowd of coaches gathered around the results. Then he jumped up and shouted with sheer jubilation. Everyone ran over, reading the results from the bottom, looking for "Salem" to show up. Had they gotten top ten? Top five? Finally, their eyes reached Salem, in the third position. They jumped and screamed and hugged and joined in a huddle of sweaty, ecstatic runners. At the center Almond was laughing, on the verge of tears. "I thought we might get a top–five finish," he yelled, "but third?!"

The teammates held each other as tightly as they could, and then fell away from each other. The boys panted not from the exertion of the race (now long–forgotten), but from the exhilaration of placing better than any of them had expected. Now Paul had only one concern left: he walked over to check if he had finished All–Ohio. He and Patrick had indeed finished in the top 25, earning second team honors. But before he could find the individual results, he decided to see who had defeated them. Obviously Edgewood took the first spot, and their team stood next to the results, stoic, as if it were no big deal to win the State Title. Under their name was none other than Cardinal Mooney, who had barely edged Salem by two points. Taking third but losing to Mooney was bittersweet; Salem had proved that they deserved to be at the meet, but not that they were better than Mooney.

Ironically, it was the Quakers who first broke the news to Mooney. Yanek spotted their rivals cooling down in the distance; the Salem boys raced toward them. "You guys came in second!" they shouted. The Mooney boys leapt into the air on legs that no longer felt tired; they were as surprised to take second as Salem's runners had been to earn third. The Quakers watched with vicarious joy. Their message to Mooney served as both a laurel and an olive branch: congratulations, we bear you no ill will. The thrill of success left no room for envy or spite.

Salem's and Mooney's celebrations left the Edgewood runners looking grim by comparison. The state champions marched off the field without smiling. They had been expecting this victory all year; its arrival had practically been preordained. Almond, who loved winning only slightly less than he loved running, could not fathom Edgewood's calm. "Guys," he addressed his own team, "Even if we take first at every meet all next season, I'm still gonna celebrate if we win State." His runners agreed. They felt this good after placing third, and winning could only be better...their brains could not quantify such euphoria. A State Championship must be the pinnacle of athletic happiness. They trotted back into the grandstands, where their fans and families were still listening for the results to come over the loudspeaker.

As the boys entered the crowd, they heard the intercom boom, "In third place, Salem High School." The Quakers followed the ensuing cheers into their parents' arms. The families took photographs, the runners chugged soda, and everyone from Salem struggled to appreciate the reality of the team's success.

After ten minutes of this bacchanalia, the loudspeaker spoke again. "The appeal period for the Boys' Division II Race is now over. The posted results are official." The Quakers laughed with relief. They had really placed third; it was official. Almost.

Paul's father drily amended the announcement. "Now we just have to wait till November 12," he said to his brother, Joe's father. Joe overheard the exchange without apprehension. He had actually forgotten about the November 12 court date, the one seeking a permanent injunction against the OHSAA. That case would be a formality, a reiteration of the Columbiana judge's first ruling in favor of Salem. His uncle sure was a worrywart.

No doubts plagued the runners that night as they traveled back home, nor during the coming week as they settled back into their everyday lives. The next mention of further controversy came at the team's banquet on the evening of November 11.

The X–tra Mile Club had bought the top eight Salem boys gray hooded sweatshirts designed by Almond. The hoodies displayed several small logos of Ohio, inside of which were written "3rd" in bold letters. This was to remind the boys that they had earned their finish, and that nothing anyone said could change that.

As it happened, the court reversed its decision the next day on November 12. The final ruling chastised the OHSAA for ignoring its own procedure, but determined that the Regional officials had acted in good faith and arrived at the accurate results. Moreover, other kids would suffer irreparable damage if Salem won the injunction – the OHSAA insisted that Cardinal Mooney would have to be disqualified if Salem's finish were made official. Salem's administrators were more than willing to accept Mooney's second–place finish; their quarrel had never been with the nearby school. But such a compromise did not occur: Salem and all its boys (save Gorby, who had qualified independently of the team) were removed from the State results, Paul's All–Ohio status was revoked, and the legal fees of both parties were charged to the Salem School District.

The OHSAA admitted no wrongdoing, but its actions suggested otherwise. Well before the 2004 cross country season began, the cross country tournament regulations were changed to eliminate the jury of appeals and provide for a standard appeal form. Most tellingly, the ten minute appeal period was abolished, allowing the results to be reviewed for up to 24 hours after their release. There would be no repeats of the 2003 controversies. The Salem school district had taken care of that, even if it had lost its case.

The runners maintained their "who cares?" attitude when they learned that they had been disqualified. So what if some piece of paper did not say that they had run at State? Each of them knew he had been there. Nothing could keep them from their memories, just as nothing could keep them from returning to State next year. And nothing could keep them from winning.

Chapter 5

The Foundation

"The will to win means nothing if you haven't the will to prepare."

– Juma Ikangaa

At first, Joe did not mind that Salem's third place finish had been erased. If a slower team or a slower runner wanted to tell himself that he had lost to a team that did not belong in Columbus, that was fine by Joe. The Quakers had met and exceeded their goal of qualifying for State. But he also wanted Salem to be clearly in the right; he did not want anyone to think that Salem had gotten some kind of unfair treatment.

Of course, some people still did. Newspaper columns, letters to the editor, and (of course) posts on JJHuddle all criticized Salem and its runners for the legal mess of 2003. Joe hated having his and his team's ethics called into question. He believed that the Quakers deserved to have raced at State, but some doubts still remained.

Moreover, State had not been everything Almond promised. At least it had not been for Joe, the sixth man, who felt he had not contributed to Salem's finish. He had not been necessary even at Districts and Regionals, where Ryan Griffith would also have beaten Mooney's sixth and broken the ties. Joe had raced passably at State, but the more he thought about his performance the less satisfied he was with it. Joe wanted a break from the questions and soul–searching, not to mention his teammates and the workouts. Now that basketball season was starting, Joe and Paul had to decide where they would place their priorities.

Almond had explained to the team the significance of year–round training, at the exclusion of all other sports. "Nothing helps running more than running does," Almond would mention in lectures over and over again. "Do you see basketball players tossing a football around? No. They practice basketball to get better at basketball." Another sport risked injuries that could leave a runner off the roads for months at a time. The answer seemed obvious; if they continued running year round, the successes would only become greater. But the decisions for Joe and Paul were not as clear–cut as they were for other members of the team.

Their fathers were two of six brothers, all of whom had played basketball at Salem and in college. When the youngest brother, Mark, finished his senior season, an era ended. *The Salem News* wrote a long story commemorating the brothers' careers, calling the Shivers boys Salem's "first family of basketball." *The New York Times* published a piece Joe's father had written about his basketball memories. By the time the youngest sister, Mary Beth, had entered SHS, the school offered a girls' basketball program. She too played four years in high school. Basketball was, and remained, an important part of the Shivers' lives. The brothers, and now their children, regularly played pick–up games together. But the second generation of Shivers basketball players had not quite panned out.

Connor, six months older and six inches taller than Joe, was the first to quit the sport. Neither he nor Joe had made the team in middle school, and both had played on the school's developmental squad. But eighth grade was it for Connor; he did not like the sport enough to harness his height and practice all summer the way his father and uncles had. He concentrated his athletic energies on recreational running, and he read prolifically in his spare time.

Joe had played the game longer than Connor. His shot was a little better and his understanding of the game was a little deeper, but he was still not very good at the sport. He could not jump, he was not quick, he was not strong, he did not see the floor well, he was not aggressive, and he handled the ball poorly. He barely made the freshman team, which cut no one. He played basketball because it was sometimes fun, and because he had never found a good reason to stop.

By ninth grade, Paul was leaning more and more towards quitting basketball. His dad had promised him, "Paul, you'll catch all of those guys in maturity by the end of your time at Salem, just like I did." But that promise seemed empty after two junior high seasons of riding the bench. He decided that his freshman year would make or break his basketball career. If he made gains on his teammates, he would pursue the sport. Otherwise, running would become his only competitive activity. Although the season provided new opportunities — five players moved up to junior varsity and varsity — Paul failed to attain his standards. Basketball was over for him, but he did not know how to break the news to his parents.

Joe barely considered running year–round. He felt obligated to continue the family legacy, and he wanted a break from Almond and the team. Paul found it easier to quit basketball with his cousin still playing: there was still a Shivers on the Salem team. Paul used his All–Ohio finish to justify his decision to his parents. He knew where his strength lay, and it was on the cross country course. Paul joined the Indoor Track program that Almond had begun this year. "Indoor" was a club, not an official sport, but it provided an excuse for Almond to hold practices with his cross country runners during the long winter.

Joe liked basketball, but some days he missed his cross country teammates. He would see Paul, Josh, Naylor, Tommy, and Yanek bundled up and running past the high school, and he would yearn to get out of the gymnasium and run until his legs lost feeling. He would wonder why he had turned away from cross country. His basketball skills barely improved throughout the season, but at least it kept him in shape. When the basketball season ended, Joe was able to rejoin his fellow runners in relatively the same place he had left off.

When Outdoor Track "conditioning" began in March under Coach Huda, Paul was torn between two different training methods. He could continue with Almond's program, which obviously worked in the cross country season, or he could follow the track program, which had raised many talented athletes to greatness. Paul knew Almond's plan was superior to the "old–school" training, but he felt a strong loyalty to the coaches who had invested in him his freshman year. Track had given Paul the opportunity to train with Shane Harding and to run in the championship meets, and it had promised Paul a bright future. On the other hand, Almond had shunned Paul at times, often focusing time and effort on Patrick, who had just come off a spectacular freshman season. At the Cross Country banquet, he even went as far as predicting that Patrick would break every Salem record from the 800m to the 5k. Those words lit a fire in Paul: he vowed to prove the prophecy wrong and to dominate the track season. Paul knew that he would receive all of the attention in track, and that would allow him to excel in his race, the 3200m.

But then Todd Huda, in his first year as boys' head coach, allowed Almond (the head of the girls' team) to coach the distance runners. The expectations were high for the distance team, especially for Patrick Gorby, who had led the cross country team to a third place finish at the State Championships. He and Aiman chose the 1600–meter (roughly a mile) as their main event, assuming that Paul was still the best 3200m runner after a solid freshman year. But after Paul injured his tail–bone in the middle of the season, they tried the longer race. Aiman bettered Paul's personal record in the race by 11 seconds, and Gorby was not far behind. The success caused them to reconsider their main race. Almond pointed them towards the 3200 when he informed them how the Region was shaping up in both that race and the 1600. He promised them that they had a much better chance of qualifying for the State meet in the 3200m; the 1600 was to be far more competitive. Unfortunately for one of Salem's three 3200 runners, a team may send only two runners per event to the District Meet. Each of the three boys who could run well enough at Districts to qualify for Regionals, and the coaches had to come up with a fair way to determine who Salem's two runners would be.

Almond decided to base his decision on two dual meets in which Paul, Aiman, and Patrick would race man–to–man–to–man to see who was the best in the event. The first race took place at Salem's Reilly Stadium against Struthers, a conference rival. Patrick won the race in a time of 10:04, edging out Paul by 3 seconds. Aiman, despite leading the race late, fell back and finished in a time of 10:15. The second race was during a dual meet a week laterIn a near–photo finish, Aiman defeated Paul: they both ran a time of 10:07. Gorby, much like Aiman had in the previous race, fell behind and finished in a time of 10:18.

The two competitions provided no conclusive evidence as to who deserved to run at Districts. Almond scored the meets, and the three teammates all came out with 4 points. Had Paul won the second race, the scores would have shifted to 3, 4, and 5, favoring Paul and Patrick. Almond and Huda were now left with a difficult decision; they had to predict which two runners would perform best in the State tournament, and which one runner would be left running the mile.

Although Paul had the best overall average time from the two races, he had the slowest personal record at 10:07. Since all the other factors were fairly even, the coaches made their decision based on PR, and chose Patrick and Aiman because they had run 10:04 and 10:01 respectively. But Paul still had the 1600m and the 4x800m to run at District, certainly not a bad consolation prize. Mike would join Paul in the mile after out–performing teammates in similar run–off meets.

In the District 4x800, Paul ran the third leg for Salem's team, which finished 4th and qualified for the Regional meet. He was not as fortunate in the mile, placing 5th despite a personal record time of 4:36. Aiman and Patrick both finished among the top 4 in the 3200m easily, but Patrick was disqualified for running inside the first lane. He had not been trying to cheat, and the officials had warned him several times, but he had stayed inside without thinking about it. Only Aiman, the third best runner in cross–country that year, would move on to the State qualifying meet.

On the Monday before Regionals, the coaches called for a 4x800 run–off. Paul had run 11 miles the day before with Aiman and knew he did not have a chance. Lance Murphy and Mike Downs, a former hurdler, easily beat the tired Paul, who now had to go to Regionals as a mere alternate. Wednesday night the 4x800 team fell short of qualifying for State when their anchor fell apart in his second lap. Despite running in second for most of the third leg, they finished seventh overall. Aiman finished 4th in the Region with a time of 9:44, a school record, but didn't fair as well at State, failing to finish in the top 10.

Salem's cross country runners expected to win the State Championship in 2004. All seven of the boys who had raced at Scioto Downs in 2003 were returning, all with confidence and experience. The consensus among them was that Almond was the best coach in the state. And few booster programs could match the X–tra Mile Club. From its athletes to its training to even the matching warm–ups given to the runners, Salem seemed invincible.

Yanek managed to dispel any of his teammates' illusions of invulnerability before summer training began. He broke his ankle. Almond warned his runners continually about taking stupid risks (i.e. playing pick–up games of basketball, jumping out of moving vehicles, etc.), because a minor tear or sprain can quickly snowball into an incapacitating injury. The boys listened to his advice selectively, allowing themselves (in

Mike and Aiman's case) backyard football games or (in Gorby's case) ATV–driving. But Yanek had not been doing anything wrong. He had been jogging to his car through the parking lot at Reilly track when he took a bad step on a curb and landed on the outside of his foot. His doctor prohibited his running for at least a month. His teammates gained new appreciation for their own vulnerability, a reality that the teenagers rarely acknowledged. And Yanek's image of his senior season fractured before it had even begun.

But Matt did not surrender. He trained vigorously in the pool, aqua–jogging for long hours. In order to bring his heart rate up to the equivalent of an easy run, Matt had to work diligently, concentrating on each rise of his knees and each swing of his arms, with his only motivation being to make varsity his senior year. The rest of the team failed to understand the hardships Matt was enduring, and even Almond ignored Salem's 5th runner, leaving him to figure out his own schedule most of the time.

The freak accident might have troubled the Quakers and their first place hopes, had they not gained a new member. Isaac Newton attended Heartland Christian Academy, the same private school in which Coach Wilson taught gym and coached basketball, and where there was no cross country program. He had been forced to race on his own all last year, though he had trained with the Salem boys occasionally. In those workouts he had stuck with the top dogs – Gorby, Paul, and Aiman – but in races he had barely beaten Joe. He exuded a sense of unrealized potential, even more so because he had been Columbiana County's top runner (and Yanek's chief rival) when he was in Middle School. Despite a personal best of just over 18 minutes, Isaac was poised to bloom as a senior.

Isaac spoke in a high, precise voice. He wore oval glasses and addressed adults politely. His grin and his manners could have identified him as one of those mild nerds who go through high school dreaming about fantasy worlds, and Isaac's passion for science fiction gave credence to that possibility. But his hair shouted otherwise; it tumbled from his scalp in curls that Isaac let do as they please. The auburn tangles showed a wild nature Isaac himself rarely indicated. The hair demanded attention so that he did not need to. He could speak as softly as he wanted without giving the impression of passivity. When he did make a crazy joke or suggest a far–fetched scheme (like living in Wal–Mart for a week), it did not seem out of character at all. The boys liked him.

Isaac Newton's transfer and Yanek's injury complicated the question of team position: the order in which the Quakers would cross the line. Last year at the State meet, Salem's runners had finished with Gorby first and Paul second, followed by Aiman, Mike, Yanek, Joe, and Ryan. Naylor, the alternate, had graduated, but the rest of Salem's State team would return for the '04 season. Almond encouraged everyone on the team to try to improve his placement relative to his teammates. Thus virtually everyone sought to advance to the next level: the junior varsity runners aspired to a top–eight spot, the eighth man coveted the seventh, the sixth and seventh jockeyed for a top–five position, and the fastest finishers battled for the honor of first on the team.

The boys out of contention for varsity spots worked no less hard because of it. Erik Cibula, the sole freshman joining the Quakers, consistently finished last in workouts. He sometimes joked about being lazy, but not many lazy teenagers would last on the Salem cross country team. Jason Stewart, one of the five boys who remained from Almond's first Salem team, was another example of someone who won few accolades from the sport. He always ran over twenty minutes; he never received individual awards. But his dedication impressed his coach and his teammates. As he worked to improve on his personal best, he inspired his faster teammates who were working to fill the team's top spots.

The eighth man on a cross–country team maintains what some might perceive to be a comfortable role. In postseason meets he enjoys all his teammates' luxuries (free food, free travel, free admission) without the anxiety of racing. But one does not become the eighth runner on a team like Salem's by being content to watch from the stands as his teammates compete. Naylor loved that his team had done so well last year, and he shared their triumphs. But always he knew that he could have run with them at State on the day of truth if he had been just a little bit faster.

The sixth and seventh runners contribute indirectly to their team's victory. Because they do not score points, they usually help only as spoilers, by displacing other teams' scorers. If Salem's sixth man were to beat another team's fifth, that fifth man would add one extra point to his team's score. But this had rarely happened last year, because Joe and Ryan had not been faster than most teams' fifth men. They had, fortunately, beaten Mooney's sixth man on two consecutive tie–breakers – relatively rare occurrences in high school cross country. Usually, the resolution of a meet depends on a team's top five runners.

The top five each score points in exactly the same way, and the only distinction between them is the order they cross the finish line. But just as complacency had not won Patrick, Paul, Aiman, Mike, and Yanek their positions at the front of the team, they were not satisfied to relax once there. Mike had worked all last year to overcome Yanek, whereupon he had set his sights on Paul. Aiman, Paul, and Patrick, meanwhile, had jockeyed for first in every race of the 2003 season. Yanek was the exception to the upward mobility that characterized his comrades; he had stagnated in the middle of that year and run poorly at State.

Almond, who had been the unchallenged number–one runner on his high school team and a clear second in college, did not discourage competition within his team. But he confused the boys with his mixed messages. Sometimes Almond would say, "It doesn't matter if your teammate beats you; it's the same number of points for Salem either way." Other times the advice was, "Sure, you wanna beat your teammates. But that doesn't mean you *hate* each other..." Whatever Almond said, there were only eight runners who earned letters, only seven who ran at State, only five who scored, and only one who would stand on the very top of the podium if the team won State. And no matter how it affected the final score, beating one of the dozens of strangers in a race did not hold the appeal of beating one of the dozen guys who had run together all season. As they started to train, the Quakers evaluated themselves and each other daily.

The star of the summer was the new runner, Isaac. He soared ahead of his teammates every time he ran with them, whether the pace was supposed to be fast or slow. On the days when the boys trained separately, he ran impossibly hard workouts with a friend from another school. Isaac's tales of ten miles in an hour awed the other Quakers. How could he not have run any faster than eighteen minutes last year? Clearly, here was a runner who could lead even a first–place state team.

Of course, his competition from the rest of Salem's runners was limited. Ryan and Mike rarely attended practice, Yanek was hurt, and Aiman and his family spent nearly a month in Morocco. Paul and Gorby, along with Mike and Aiman, had competed in late–season track meets. Thus, their summer training began later than Isaac's. Besides that, both were hampered by injuries – Paul by hip pain and Gorby by a host of temporary, unrelated ailments.

This discouraging beginning to cross country did not help Patrick Gorby forget the abrupt and unfortunate end to his track season. He had always been able to outperform his teammates in the same way he had run inside the line at the District Track Meet: naturally, without thinking. Last cross country season he had finished first in the Metro Athletic Conference championship meet, held on Salem's course. His father, who rode his ATV ahead of all the races at Memorial Park, had let Patrick take a victory lap and lead the girls' race. Then the boy had further celebrated when his mother brought cake to Memorial Park. Why the cake? It was Patrick's birthday. It was natural that he should finish first on his team and first in the race, and natural that he win himself a medal on his birthday.

The events of May and June disrupted the natural order. Had not Almond predicted that Patrick would be individual state champion by his senior year? How could Isaac Newton, whom Gorby had beaten by over a minute last year, now be besting him effortlessly on every hard run? Why was he not fast anymore? Patrick had lost the confidence that sprung him to the lead of races, workouts, and the team. Without it, he gave in to the pain more often, falling back on runs he would have led the year before. Some felt that Almond had built him up too high, leaving the boy to come crashing down at the first sight of adversity. Gorby needed to be pushed and hardened just as much as any other runner on the team.

By mid–July, only one of Salem's runners had consistently come close to Isaac. Joe Shivers was coming off a track season in which he had performed better than in any previous athletic endeavor. He used the spring to establish the mood for the summer, and pursued Isaac with all the enthusiasm he had. Joe felt stronger and faster than he ever had. Throughout his adolescence he had lost in all manner of sports to kids who were more physically mature: quicker, bigger, and with more testosterone–fueled aggression. Maybe now Joe was finally reaping the benefits that his father, who had grown three–and–a–half inches after turning sixteen, had promised him.

The first true workout in July epitomized the team's status. The runners were to jog out to a loop known as "Pennsylvania," named after the desolate street that made up the majority of the loop. After the short two–mile warmup, everyone would begin a three to four–mile workout at a difficult pace. The Quakers wore heart monitors purchased by the X–tra Mile Club, and Almond used the runners' heart rates to classify workout runs as either "hard" or "anaerobic threshold." On hard days the boys' heartbeats stayed under 175 beats per minute – an intense but sustainable level of effort. Anaerobic threshold (A.T.) runs were spent between 175 and 185 beats per minute, when the body accumulates lactic acid and suffers cramps.

Almond did not quantify how difficult today's run was supposed to be, but he knew it would be hard. This would be the first true workout that Paul, Gorby, and Mike Overholser had completed since track season, and their coach knew that the runners had grown tired of their easy preseason jogs. Isaac and Joe, further advanced in their training, considered today just another run. But for Paul and Patrick especially, it was their first chance to test their bodies in months. Tension built through all fifteen minutes of the warm–up, and then the run truly began.

Patrick set a brutal pace down the initial hill; Paul stayed in the back of the pack, waiting for the pace–setter to tire. As they reached the mile mark of the run, Patrick was already fading, and Mike had fallen back quite a bit. Joe, Isaac, and Paul remained strong and continued the pace onto Pennsylvania Avenue on the outskirts of Salem. The road was ideal for running because few cars traveled on its two–mile stretch and there was plenty of grass on the roadside in case a car did come. Pennsylvania also had very little shade and very little scenery to distract from the exercise. By two–and–a–half miles into the workout, Patrick Gorby had realized he was not the fittest person there. As he ran by a driveway into a construction company's parking lot, Patrick fell.

The other three boys came to an abrupt halt. "What happened?" Isaac asked Patrick. "Are you all right?"

"I hurt my hip," answered Patrick, rubbing his side. Paul rolled his eyes. He wondered if Gorby had staged the fall to get out of the workout. But Paul was hurting too, so he welcomed the opportunity to take a quick rest. Patrick stood up slowly. "You guys go on without me," he insisted. "I'll jog back.".

Now the group had dwindled down to just three runners, two of whom felt great. Paul, on the other hand, was suffering miserably. He barely hung with the team's fittest athletes for the duration of Pennsylvania, and he prayed that the stoplight at the end of the road would be red. To his dismay, it was green, and the three continued up a long gradual hill. They reached the summit on Second Street, a continuation of Pennsylvania into town, and strode to the finish a couple hundred meters further. Gasping for air, Paul put his hands on his knees and hunched over. Isaac, fresh as he had been 30 minutes earlier, jogged over to a fast food restaurant to grab Paul a cup of water while Joe remained with his cousin. Paul poured the water over himself, and the three made their way back to the high school. Patrick limped in after a little while, followed by two more teammates. Mike had fallen from the lead group halfway through the run and managed to finish alongside Justin Roberts, known to his team and schoolmates as "Stogus".

How he had gotten the nickname was a mystery; not even Justin himself was sure exactly who first christened him or when. It was not the most flattering name, but Stogus was good at turning frustrations into fuel for his running. He was having an amazing summer, finishing workouts in the top seven continually. No one knew what his capabilities were, since he had joined the team only last year. Paul was the first to classify Stogus as a potential sixth or seventh runner, which only fueled his ambition. Finishing beside Mike today boosted him further, and the workout also left Joe feeling confident: it was the closest he had finished to Paul in years. Paul was happy for his cousin, but worried that he himself was behind the curve. If Isaac could run this fast this early in the summer, Paul had a lot of ground to make up.

He and the other Quakers traversed all of Salem's training courses: the desolate Pennsylvania, the hilly Butcher, the quiet Pine Lake, and the brutal Painter Hill. As the team's hierarchy grew more defined, Isaac never acknowledged that he was beating his new teammates every day; apparently he saw no reason for surprise. Joe, on the other hand, could not accept that he was Salem's number–two man. He felt sure that he would return to the sixth spot, where there was no real pressure, soon enough: when Aiman returned to the US, when Paul and Patrick caught up with their training, and when Mike started coming to practice everyday.

Paul spent the majority of the summer trying to gain his coaches' respect. Every piece of hard work he put towards running was fueled by the attention he was not receiving. He wanted desperately to be like Patrick Gorby, to be liked by his coaches. Words of advice were gospel to Paul; if Almond told the team to be better teammates, Paul went out of his way to say "Good job!" to each and everyone of his fellow runners. He tried to be a leader, but he ultimately failed because the team had far too many conflicting personalities.

Mike and Aiman comprised the biggest problem to any potential team leader. They disdained authority and often worked together to tear down the head of the team. Alone, each controllable and passive. But together they argued against one victim, overwhelming their opponent with a continuous verbal barrage. After quickly realizing leadership was a stretch, Paul tried to earn his teammates' respect by example.

The most memorable run of Paul's summer was also one of his worst. The team went for a hard run on Egypt Road, which ran across the bottom of Painter Hill. Paul felt terrible, sick, and uninterested the whole run as he watched his teammates pass him one by one. His pace slowed to a jog up the steep hill, and he managed his way back to the high school after rejoining his team at the top of Painter. There was little he could have done to run a better workout; he was ill and could not help that. But his teammates had run incredibly well, something to which he had never really paid much attention before.

During the post–workout meeting, Paul decided to take the stage. "Guys, I had a terrible workout today," he said as Almond looked on with curiosity. "But I saw ten other guys run fantastic workouts and kill themselves for the team. So I have to say that today was a good workout, because the team improved." Almond was stunned. He had perceived the boy as spoiled and self–centered. The speech surprised Almond, but it was not an epiphany for Paul. Fe had run for his team in the past, shared success with them, and been happy for their accomplishments. But now he was buying in completely, committing one–hundred percent to Salem, and keeping Paul Shivers's success off his list of priorities. Paul made the statement for Almond, to show him that Paul was no longer running for himself.

During late July Mike took a seemingly endless vacation at his aunt's house in Columbus. This holiday was harmless at first, but as it dragged on Almond grew worried about the boy he believed to be the key to the team's success. He doubted that Mike would follow his training plan or even run at all while he stayed in Columbus. Without its fifth man in shape, Salem would be out of contention for a State title. Almond finally contacted Mike's mother concerning his whereabouts, and he was informed that Mike would be home in two days. A rumor quickly spread among the team that Mike intended to quit cross country and instead play golf. A melodramatic Almond ordered the boys to go to Mike's house and give him two options: party and be lazy, or run for Salem cross country.

The irony of the whole situation was that Mike actually had no intention of quitting the team. Paul telephoned the returning Mike, who dismissed Almond's worries. The story that he was going to quit was basically a lie to keep Almond from calling him. The mercurial Overholser would be racing alongside them this year; they did not even need to confront him. So, the mission to Mike's house became a cordial one – everyone pitched in for pizza, and they ate it in his kitchen. If their intent had ever been to draw a line with Mike, they failed. The overall effect was of awkward appeasement, and it served to amuse Mike more than impress him with friendship. He learned again what he had already known: he was an essential part of their State championship hopes, and the Quakers would tolerate his antics and games if he showed up for races.

Mike returned in time to complete the roster of the Salem Cross Country team as it headed to Camp Wakonda for the second year. Camp was one of the changes Almond had not had time to institute in his first year, when he had not been hired until late July. Like the ten–mile fundraiser run that the boys and girls undertook in July, Camp Wakonda was a summer tradition that Almond had introduced to popular approval from his athletes.

Camp Wakonda lay an hour away in Carroll County, removed from any humanity but the family that ran the facility. Its name made it seem more exotic than its tranquil forest trails and well–lit bathrooms did, but the campground got the Quakers far enough out of their comfort zones for Almond's purposes. The runners did the bulk of their training on the deserted road that was the only way into camp, a route hilly enough to be legendary. But Wakonda's geography was not the point, either. Even in flat Salem there were roads where the runners could train just as hard. The purpose of the camp, as Almond told the kids repeatedly, was to bring them together. Four nights in a cabin full of bunk beds ought to unify the boys. Or drive them crazy.

The runners shared the first two days of camp with Salem's middle school teams, a fact that only added to the high schoolers's stress. Both groups stayed in the same red wooden buildings, and both groups ran together. Most of the younger kids did not or could not keep up with the veterans, but they all tried to prove themselves to their role models. J.D. Winkler and Thomas Clunen showed off their speed in front of the high school runners. The Floor twins, Brandon and Jason, showed promise, as did Lance Murphy's brother Brian, Tommy Yuhaniak's brother Ted, and Joe's brother Brian. Salem Cross Country had a devoted if small crop of prospects coming up next year. And if these kids seemed less refined than the Quakers could remember themselves being at that age, they were also faster.

Normally the middle school kids would follow their own training program, but camp was an anomaly in the precise Salem training plan. Almond told his runners to "go how you feel," but he clearly wanted them to push harder than usual. He fondly described his college camp, where he and his teammates had amused themselves by exhausting their bodies with as much exercise and as little sleeping as possible. The coach did not punish anyone for running easy, but the majority of the boys kicked off the camp with a run of twelve or more miles, the most they had run at one time.

Mike dominated the runs at camp. He survived the brutal twelve–miler on Sunday and woke up the next morning ready for a hard run. He, Paul, and Aiman took the run out fast, too sleepy to realize how fast they were going. Paul felt as if he were floating through the foggy woods, but as the run drew on and he became more awake, the pain set in. His bleary eyes focused on the boy steadily pulling away from him. Mike's short legs and quick foot turnover gave him a tiny stride that looked like a clumsy shuffle. His arms, mirroring his choppy steps, sat high on his chest and barely swung back and forth. His face turned as red as it did during his fits of laughter, but not a glimmer of pleasure shone from his eyes. In fact, Mike's whole face seemed dead, as though his body could not maintain anything but his motoring legs. He did not look much like a conditioned athlete, but eventually he broke away from Paul and Aiman, proving he was in decent shape.

After three–and–a–half miles the three boys turned around toward camp, and Mike increased his lead. On the way back Paul saw Almond and Wilson, who were still heading out along the road. Paul sucked in a breath just before passing

Almond. "Yeah," he gasped sarcastically. "Mike isn't in shape."

Each of the three full days the Quakers were at camp, they had the option of running twice a day. Paul exhausted most of his remaining energy in swimming races at the lake, so he chose to take it easy on Monday's afternoon run. Some went on longer, tougher runs in the afternoon, but Almond cautioned them not to overdo it. Injuries promised little fun and even less running. Matt Yanek and Tommy Yuhaniak, both recovering from ankle problems, biked on the roads and "aqua–jogged" in the lake. Matt had not been allowed to run for roughly two months, and his latest doctor's appointment was scheduled for midway through the week. Matt had not been able to keep himself from running a little, but he had eventually realized that he needed to heal before he could return. Tommy had yet to learn that lesson. He cajoled Almond into letting him run, then went twenty minutes beyond what the coach had advised. His ankle swelled up, and he was back to the bike.

Tommy and Matt were not the only injury–plagued Salem runners. Both Aiman and Paul were noticing significant hip pain after runs. The steep downhills on the old roads aggravated the developing runners, so Almond prescribed ice, aspirin, and fewer miles. Fortunately, the two were still able to complete training runs without being hindered by the pain. Paul and Aiman became closer while sitting together icing their wounds. Both stood tall and lanky, both had run similar times in Track and Cross Country, and now both dealt with hip pain. A stranger might have thought these superficial resemblances would make pair nearly identical runners. But their personalities and race strategies differed in ways that would become more and more obvious throughout the year.

Similarly, Joe considered Mike his opposite. Joe faithfully followed the rules (in running and in society), and ran exactly as long and hard as Almond recommended. Mike's lifestyle, on the other hand, allowed for bursts of indulgence, like staying up late with girls the night before State or his partying binge of this summer, during which he had gained several pounds. But his runs blazed out of control, too: he had ended his stay in Columbus with consecutive days of intense workouts, and the day before camp started he had run ten miles on his own. Joe experienced giddiness at the end of hard runs, and everything around him seemed to radiate joy. But Mike became philosophical after workouts; he wondered aloud about how much more humanity could accomplish by cooperating.

Of course Mike's calm lasted no longer than Joe's lightheartedness: when their endorphins disappeared, their normal personalities returned. Mike's normal personality could be brash and loud. The runners' exhaustion and physical proximity did little to improve their patience. Mike and Andy Thompson, another junior, were the first to fight openly. By Tuesday afternoon, Mike had provoked Andy one too many times without reason, and Andy had threatened Mike one too many times without backing himself up. Andy swung at the smaller boy, who retaliated only with hysterical laughter and emerged from the scuffle red–faced. Neither was hurt, and their coaches did not see what had happened. But as the boys began their afternoon runs, they were still recounting the incident.

Yanek, Isaac, and Joe ran recovery laps in Wakonda's wooded trails as they reflected on the day's events. The more they talked, the more they blew the brief scuffle out of proportion. Of all the Quakers, these three probably held the most idealized views of Cross Country. Joe, to whom academic success came as a given, saw the sport as the most challenging and therefore most meaningful part of his life. Isaac, who had never felt such acceptance from teammates, resolved to mend this rift before it ruined Salem's season. While at camp he had shaved his head; the Quakers were making a mark on him. And Yanek, also a senior, had not spent the past two months aqua–jogging and dreaming of recovery to watch his team destroy itself. In fact, today was his first run since his injury.

Matt Yanek had begun running cross country as an eighth grader, when he learned that his muscular body was faster than those of the typical featherweights who took up the sport. When he had entered high school he had found himself outmatched by upperclassmen like Robert Vogt and Shane Harding, and he tried to learn from them to improve his own performance (going as far as incorporating Vogt's trademark hitch into his stride). But when he served as Shane's right–hand man in 2002 (even leading Salem while Shane was sidelined with an injury), it was the height of his individual success. His physical maturity had peaked when he was in middle school; the young runners behind him had been closing the gap ever since. In 2003 Patrick, Paul, and Aiman all beat him by a wide margin, and Mike edged him out at State. Yanek's broken ankle in 2004 might have been the melancholy cap on his career.

But Yanek had long since put his team's glory ahead of his own, and now he wanted only to be a part of the Quakers' 2004 varsity squad. As his friends had run and he had toiled in the pool, he longed to join them and run again. No matter how dull a run became, it would shine compared to his hours and hours of weight–lifting. No matter how obnoxious his teammates acted on a certain day, he would cherish every minute that was not spent in solitude. Yanek's recovery into running shape excited him with all the energy he had expended to achieve it. Now he turned this energy to resolving what he saw as a crisis in his team. He formed an emergency plan.

When the three returned to their cabin, they called for a meeting of the boys' team. Since the Middle School team had left the previous day, the Quakers had moved to a single cabin, so it did not take long to assemble them all outside.

Once the boys convened, however, nobody had much useful to say. They looked at the sky and their feet, and the impetus behind the meeting evaporated. The confrontation now appeared more like an isolated clash of tempers than a symptom of a cancer destroying the team. Mike and Andy mumbled apologies to each other and reluctantly shook hands. The meeting finished awkwardly, accomplishing little, but not making the situation worse. With the crisis (or at least the perception of one) averted, the boys could concentrate on the important business of pestering the girls' team.

On Tuesday night, the second–to–last night of camp, the boys planned a water balloon raid on the girls' cabin. Although Almond had threatened immediate removal from camp for any such misbehavior, the guys were still forming strategies. Mike and Aiman were the ringleaders of the operation, and would leave the campfire early on to get into position on top of the girls' cabin. Paul, Isaac, Matt, Josh, and Patrick were going to attack the girls with balloons, and when they would try to reenter their cabin, Mike and Aiman would hit them from above. Everyone else was considered "defense." The leaders told them that it was imperative that they stay back and defend the cabin with water balloons. In fact, it was to keep them out of the way.

The year before, the boys had performed a similar raid, which was not very successful. The girls had reciprocated, dumping buckets of water on the guys while they were sleeping. Mike had not taken too kindly to the clandestine attack, and had proceeded to blast a hose through the girls' screen door. Nothing was ruined, but Almond warned the team that nothing of the sort would take place in 2004.

The 2004 operation started off poorly when Mike and Aiman failed to scale the girls' cabin. The main attackers began the assault, but were soon thwarted when the girls locked themselves in the bathroom, taunting their attackers. Paul and Gorby took up positions in the woods as the excitement died down, only to find Almond there with a large inflatable green alien. He had been planning to hide in the woods and that he planned to use to scare the girls. The coach told them to leave, which forced the two to put their brilliant plan into motion immediately. As soon as the girls finally left the bathroom to go back to the cabin, Paul and Patrick sprung from the woods and tossed several balloons at the screaming girls. The girls took only splashes, and no direct hits, since the throws were rushed. After the boys had gone back to their cabins, Almond implemented his attempt to scare the girls. He was mildly successful, getting a few frightened yells.

Ever vigilant for the inevitable counterattack, the boys slept lightly. At one in the morning, Almond woke up anyone that had managed to fall asleep and told them that the team was doing a night run. He passed out glow sticks to both teams and they started off down the long, unlit road. The most anyone ran was 4 miles; the idea of the run was basically to have a good time. After finally getting into bed, both teams slept soundly, with no further raids.

On Wednesday morning, Almond woke the teams at nine o'clock, instead of the usual seven, so they could make up for lost sleep. The boys took to playing poker after breakfast, and soon realized that the girls were nowhere to be found. They began joking that the girls were trashing their cabin, and not being very secretive about it. When the girls finally came back to the mess hall, the guys walked down to find that the girls had done just that. The cabin was a disaster scene. Toothpaste, shaving cream, and clothes were strewn across the dirty floor. Most of the guys' underwear were in a pile, covered in mud and toothpaste. "Served" (as in "You got served," a phrase Mike had used excessively throughout camp), was written with shaving cream on the wall. Paul gathered the angry team together, and suggested that they get revenge. He had not condoned any pranks this year, but if the girls were not afraid to make the first move, then he had to have revenge. Matt, having run out of clean underwear, was probably the most irritated.

The boys marched up to the coaches' cabin and asked politely to have the girls removed from camp. Almond's reply was simple, "There's only one day left, I can't kick them out now." The guys warned him that the girls' raid would be avenged, to which he did not say anything. Initially, Paul came up with the idea of sending the girls' belongings across the lake in a boat, but Almond did not allow them to take the boats to the beach. The next best plan was trash the girls' cabin, but Almond preemptively moved them to the nurse's cabin, which had a lock. Both teams went swimming that afternoon, except for Aiman, Mike, Matt, and Isaac, who stayed back to repay the girls in kind. Almond sent Patrick up to prevent any misbehavior, but Patrick only enabled the prank. He was lifted into a back window and then opened the door for his comrades. They tossed snacks and clothes across the floor, wrote a taunting message in lipstick on the bathroom mirror, and spilled sunscreen in the entryway.

Almond called a meeting at the boys' cabin upon surveying the girls' cabin. He lambasted the boys for "going too far"; an opinion they did not share. Even Paul thought the raid was minor compared to the damage done to the boys' cabin. Matt voiced his thoughts, which was a huge mistake considering Almond was as angry as the runners had ever seen him. Yanek said what all of the guys were thinking, that the girls deserved it. Almond told Yanek basically to shut up, and demanded that the boys clean up their cabin and the bathroom so the teams would be allowed back the following year.

The girls were angry at the guys, and they exaggerated the extent of the harm done to their new cabin. During the nightly meeting in the mess hall, the mood remained unchanged. Though the boys had come together as a team, the coaches and the girls were both livid about the situation. In order to remedy the bad feelings between the two teams, Almond called for volunteers to come up and speak to their teammates about running, teamwork, and good examples set by teammates. This allowed the teams to mend their relationship and apologize for the pranks and raids. The girls also bonded as a team as they each stood up and talked about the State meet and how they would do anything to reach their goals. Even the quiet freshmen, Liz Shivers and Sarah Yerkey, gave inspirational speeches. The emotion spread to the guys' team when Isaac thanked the boys for making him a part of their team. The thought of having training partners and teammates who cared about him brought tears to his eyes.

Almond admitted that the low point of the summer had brought the teams closer together than ever before, which was the basic idea of having a camp. Each party decided to forgive and forget, and the night ended with a team break led by the coach.

The last day of camp consisted of a nine–mile hard run. Almond had planned most of the week towards a successful last day and stressed to the runners that this run was the most important of the week. Paul knew from the start that his hip was going to be a severe problem, rendering his long stride useless. Every downhill step shot bursts of pain through his hip, preventing him from keeping up with Aiman and, eventually, the rest of the team. Mike was clearly tired from his first week of legitimate training in a while, and fell back with Paul. The two reduced the pace to a jog and chatted the entire 9 miles, often forced to slow down further due to laughter. When they arrived back at camp, Patrick and Lance were running sprints up and down a field with Almond shouting at them to run faster. The team filled Paul and Mike in on the situation; the two sprinters had run too slowly in the workout, and were being punished with sprints. Gorby seemed to be rising under the harsh treatment, but Lance looked as if every stride was his last. Almond finally ended the sprints and focused his attention on Paul and Mike. He started the conversation irate, ready to send both of them to the sprint field. But Paul explained his injury, which ironically matched Aiman's, and the conservative coach offered solutions to the problem and forgot about the slow workout.

The highlight of the run was Josh Matthews' excellent performance, finishing among the top 5 for the first time all summer. He was ecstatic and confident. Now he tried to take over leadership of the team, as recommended by Almond. He rounded his teammates up for a break, and they all understood what he was attempting. But the team was full of rebels: not mavericks, but runners who did not want to take orders from one another. They wanted to be a team, and Matthews' leadership role soon fizzled out.

Once they were back in Salem, the boys ran lightly for a few days as they prepared themselves for the onset of school. Stogus, Erik Cibula, Jason Stewart, and Joe all played in the high school band, so they marched across the parking lot every weekday morning. Cross country camp kept them (except for Jason, who left early) from attending the first couple of band practices, and once the boys returned to Salem, their runs interrupted the hours of brassy arrangements of rock classics. Even hard workouts were less painful than endless repetitions of somewhat–recognizable "blasts from the past." The scheduling conflict foreshadowed the full fall that awaited each of the Quakers. It was one thing to log easy miles in the summer, another thing altogether to work out after six hours in the classroom.

One benefit of the regimented band camp was the structure it gave the boys' days: wake up, go to band camp, run, come back to band, eat lunch, finish rehearsing and go home. The regularity droned on for all four Quakers, and even the non–bandsmen sensed the impending school year. The indolent summer meetings were falling into the rhythm of autumn. All the runners knew what they would be doing each day before Almond told them. Thursday was a long run, and Tuesday and Friday were for recovery miles. Monday was always a workout. So Almond surprised the Quakers on the 16th when he told them that they would be running easy. They pondered this under the tree on their grass island until he called them down to a field along F.E. Cope Drive, further from the blaring trumpets monopolizing the parking lot.

Almond announced that he had entered them in a fun race held that night in Boardman, on the same course as the Regional meet. The boys were astonished. Had not Almond said they

---

had run at Boardman too often last year and made it mundane? Had he not told his runners they would visit that course only once this year? Was it not early in the season for a race?

Aiman broke the tension. He whipped his shirt around his head, and shouted: "I'm 'onna win it!" His boast, in a voice modeled after comedian Dave Chappelle's, reminded the boys that this was nothing serious. Aiman was still Aiman, still full of arrogance and exuberance. His teammates followed his example; as they began running Paul described how good he felt, how ready he was to race.

Three o' clock found the girls and boys sitting in the familiar spot where their tent had stood ten months ago. There were fewer teams at this preseason meet, and no runners wore school uniforms, but otherwise the days were almost identical: Regionals last year had been unseasonably hot and sunny. And there were other similarities. Cardinal Mooney's and Edgewood's runners were there. Both teams had graduated seniors, and neither school was predicted to be as good as it had been, but today's race would show the Salem boys how they stacked up against the only two teams that had beaten them at State.

Joe warmed up with more calm than he had expected. This was just a fun race, after all, and racing is just running fast. Joe had been running fast all summer, so this was nothing new. He could do this. Racing had been such an ordeal for him last year, but today it seemed like the simplest thing in the world. He knew how bad he would feel if he raced poorly, and he planned to have a good time with his team after the race. Joe promised himself that he would beat Yanek, Josh, and Justin, and headed for the line feeling light without his usual mental baggage.

Isaac led his teammates from the first half–mile to the finish; his time (in the low 17s) would have beaten Patrick's at last year's Regional meet. Not only had he beaten his own best time by over a minute before the season even began, he had talked to other racers the whole time. Aiman trailed close behind. Joe came in at 18:11, the fastest he had ever run a cross–country course, and he beat Patrick and Paul. Paul had run a slow time; he moped for the rest of the night, and when anything minor went wrong (like a delay in being seated at the restaurant where the Quakers went afterward) he sighed, "It's just an eighteen–thirty kind of day."

The next day at the high school, before the boys began their slow run, Almond lectured them about the race.

"Now I need to say some things," he began. "You can cry if you need to; I'm gonna be a jerk." The boys turned their attention completely over to their coach's cool voice. Almond turned to Isaac.

"You guys better be thankful you have him, 'cause he just P.R.'d by a minute, in *August*, at *Boardman*." His voice rose in pitch and volume, and it emphasized his youthful joy. Almond seemed to live to appreciate displays of running like that.

"My wife likes you," Almond complimented Aiman. The coach had lost none of the warmth he had shown Isaac. "She said to me last night, after the race, 'He'll never let his team down,' and I agreed. I said, 'He never races bad.' You made some late–race moves, you were still moving in on people in the last four hundred. But you didn't kick. You out–kicked Gorby at County," he groused, referring to Track season, "And you haven't kicked since! Kick!" He grabbed Aiman's skinny shoulders and shook him, a gesture he would not have made with many of the Quakers. But the two were close, and the coach knew that Aiman would laugh rather than recoil.

"Paul, why'd you start slow and then look back to see what was going on behind you? Are you that confident? Get up front; you belong there." Almond then spoke at length about one of Paul's best track races, urging him to repeat that performance. Paul soaked in the compliments about his past races. Of course he needed to be yelled at for a poor race, but when Almond reminisced about Paul's old races, the junior felt that he had gained the respect and concern of his coach. It left Paul motivated and excited about the season ahead of him. Then he referred to the fact that Joe had beaten Paul in a race for the first time ever. "They're cousins, so what? There shouldn't be any anger within a family, that's stupid stupid stupid. What about twins who are awesome, do they fight every time one beats the other? Besides, I'm not convinced that Joe *is* a better runner, it's still early in the season."

"Gorby," he said to Patrick's drawn face, "That's gotta be the first eighteen minute 5K of your life. Am I right?" Almond was still cheerful, and he treated Patrick's soft "yeah" as an enthusiastic assent. "Pffff," the coach blew through his lips. "*That's* never gonna happen again. You're good enough that you could break every Salem record there is." Then he added, in a contradiction that he did not notice at all, "Don't feel under pressure to do great things, just have fun. Look at Aiman," and the boys glanced at their teammate's wild curls and carefree smile. Almond continued, now focusing on the older, taller boy: "He's one of the dumbest runners I know. What were you thinking before the race? 'I'm gonna go out there and tear it up.' You weren't worried about time, or place, or how you were gonna do. You just had fun." Almond advocated running "stupid", or in other words, racing without worry or strategy. If someone has trained hard enough, racing should be the easy part.

Now Almond turned to Yanek, and his tone became harsher than it had yet. This was what he had meant when he had said he would be a jerk. "Did you really think you'd run seventeen–ten? You've been running for six days. You should be mature enough to realize that you might not be in shape until Districts. Don't share your grief with your team, they know you ran bad." Yanek nodded quickly, keeping his head and eyes down. It seemed like Almond was harder on him than on anyone, but now was not the time for Yanek to question his coach.

"Gebs," he started, and Josh's dark eyes met his own. "Gebs" was short for Hailie Gebressailassie, the world champion Ethiopian whose build resembled Josh's. Almond had given Josh the nickname, and it represented Josh's aspirations for greatness. Both he and his coach knew how intensely Josh longed for a varsity spot his senior year, and both knew how intensely he would have to fight for one. "You're gonna be on the bubble again. The last half mile took you off varsity. It's the same way it's been the past three years. It's the same way it was last season, and Ryan's gonna beat you."

Ryan Griffith wanted varsity too, and he did not mind trailing Gebs for two–and–a–half miles if he could beat the older boy in a sprint. Whichever of them was faster this year, it would not be because the other had gotten worse. "You two blew my mind," exclaimed Almond. "You ran a minute faster than at Regionals last year."

"Coach," smiled Josh, "I wasn't *at* Regionals last year." Josh gave his trademark chuckle. He could laugh about his disappointments; this year he knew he would do better. This year they would all do better.

Chapter 6

The Favorites

"I don't meet competition. I crush it."
— *Charles Revson*

The Salem Cross Country Team sat and stewed in the high school parking lot. Occasionally someone would look off into the distance and sigh, but mostly they huddled in small, sleepy groups. This morning, their first "away" meet, would have passed groggily even if everything went as planned. Seven o' clock comes early on Saturday mornings during the school year, and a quiet bus ride makes it harder to dispel mental cobwebs. That difficulty would be welcome now; a boring bus is better than no bus at all. And that was what they had. Almond called the athletic director, the bus garage, and anyone else he hoped could fix the problem. He got nowhere. The boys and girls watched him, scanned the horizon for their phantom bus, and glanced at their watches. Even if the bus came right now, it would be hard for them to make it on time to the Maplewood Invitational in Cortland, Ohio, forty miles north of Salem.

"What, is this the second time the school screwed up getting a bus for us?" one runner asked. "The football team gets a ride down to the stadium for home games, and we can't get a bus a few times a year to go an hour away." In 2002 the boys had had to carpool to the Boardman Regional because no bus was provided.

"All right, guys," Almond called his team to order. "I've been calling all around, and it doesn't look like there's a bus

---

coming. There's a race up in Marlington, though." Almond's wife coached for the Marlington Schools, located twenty miles west of Salem in Alliance. "My wife knows the meet director, and he got us a spot in a race. We should be able to make it in time. Who can drive up there?""

A rush to the cars ensued: those who were over sixteen could drive themselves; those younger (including the middle school squad) had to find rides from the older kids or parents. One by one the vehicles deserted the parking lot. A school bus arrived ten minutes later to find no passengers.

The caravan arrived unharmed, ten minutes before the girls had to race. The girls had time to jog to the bathroom and the starting line. The boys had more time to warm up, but not the usual hours of acclimation to the course. Almond preached about handling adversity to his team, fueling their will to run well. The runners wanted to prove to themselves and each other that they could perform well in a difficult situation. They laughed off the circumstances; they were still here to win – though this meet was smaller than the one they had scheduled in Maplewood. None of the teams lining up beside them knew how badly they were about to be beaten.

Gorby started with the leaders, but the rest of the team moved up gradually. Talking to their teammates as they saw them, Aiman and Isaac ran side by side through the field of spikes and singlets. Joe, who had decided before the race to run the first mile with Mike, held even with the fiery runner. Paul settled into a conservative pace early. "Easy Matt, just pace out this first mile. You don't need to waste energy yet," Paul recommended to Yanek as the senior fell into stride with him. Although the pace felt leisurely, the Quakers put 7 runners through the mile in under 5:20, a major accomplishment considering the rate would lead to a sub 16:40 performance. Mike, panicked by Joe's presence, hung a few yards behind Aiman as they all entered a forest. *What are they doing?* Paul thought to himself. *They went out way too fast if they're still ahead of me.* Paul forced himself by them on one of the wooded path's steep downhills. His deceptive efforts worked: by surging past them he made himself seem too fast and strong to catch.

Joe abandoned the pace and Mike slowed down after another minute or so. As Paul battled for position, Joe watched a dozen or more runners pass him. He did not put up a fight. Joe had planned to stay with Mike in order to run intelligently, but as a result, they had both opened the first 6 minutes of the race entirely too fast.

Paul gradually moved up relative to his teammates, casting a line to Isaac as soon as he caught sight of him; he had been able to reel him in for most of the latter part of the race. But just as he was about to pull his teammate out of the water and remove the hook, Isaac dropped the line and darted away to the finish.

Aiman crossed the line second overall, upset because his supercilious race attitude had allowed a Marlington runner to disappear early in the race without his notice. Isaac's reign as leader of the team had ended, but his incredible kick enabled him to maintain a top-two spot. Patrick stumbled through the chute close behind. Paul finished fourth on the team, but he was closing the gap. Mike's first mile had deflated his tires, and the next two miles were torturous. Ryan, who had again ridden Geb's coattails for 95% of the race, used his fresh legs to pass Josh and catch Joe in the final stretch. A frustrated Josh came in eighth, and Yanek, still behind the fitness curve, finished ninth.

The boys dominated the other teams there, just as they had known they would. No one did anything surprising: times were good considering the heat. "I checked some of the other results. You guys would have won Maplewood easily, and taken first at the Hoover Invite in Division I," Almond told the guys' team at their post–race lunch The Quakers added another plate of confidence to the armor they would need to prepare themselves for a state championship.

The real legacy of the Marlington race stemmed from Almond's last–second choice to run there at all. Almond could rely on his runners to tolerate and enjoy his impulsive choices and the resulting experiences. The parents, however, preferred that the schedule be followed as written – especially the family members who had driven straight to Maplewood and waited there in vain. The middle school parents bristled at the thought of their children riding in the back seat of some high schooler's junker. And while everyone affiliated with the team (parents included) placed most of the blame on the bus–end of the problem, there was no face to associate with a scheduling error. They all knew Almond, and most of them already had a beef with him about something (an injured child, the antics at camp, or merely his abrupt manner).

To Almond, the affair read like another chapter in his losing battle against the world. He taught his runners to cheat injury by avoiding the hard sidewalks, but homeowners called the school if his runners strayed onto their lawns and motorists complained if they wove into the street. Longtime officials automatically disliked him a) because he was new to the area, and b) because he behaved toward them more like a busy high school runner would than a courteous middle–aged coach. Last year's postseason debacle had made him no friends among members of the OHSAA, and would probably taint their relationship for years. Almond knew he was not the most likable guy on earth; he admitted that his people–skills lacked polish, that his decision–making skills evinced inexperience, and that his grammatical skills often made his "Coaches Comments" painful to read. He knew that, but he did not care much. He aimed to coach a winning team, and so far he had succeeded. He did not need the world's approval any more than his team did.

Some of the team members began to associate Almond primarily with his negative qualities, and they forgot the success he had provided them. Paul could not understand their thinking: Almond had turned the program around, given his runners endless opportunity, and been there for the team during the winter and summer days that many coaches use to relax. Paul had had his disagreements with his coach, and at times he flat–out hated running, but the arguments stemmed from trivial situations that both of them were able to forget. Ultimately, Paul gave Almond the credit for all of his accomplishments, the team's accomplishments, and the change in his own attitude towards the sport. Almond was hired to build the best cross country program in the state, and so far he was doing just that.

Almond grew especially close to Mike and Aiman, and became like the big brother that neither boy had. He did his best to guide them and to keep them out of trouble, which was not an easy task. Aiman and Mike had little respect for him until the 2004 season, when he revealed his lighter side to them. He told them tales of his high school and college days, which gave Aiman and Mike a way to relate to him. They stopped looking at Almond as a slave–driving coach and instead included him as a friend, a person to whom they could talk without inhibition.

Meanwhile some of the boys, like Yanek and Ryan Griffith, felt that they could do nothing right in their coach's eyes. A typical easy day of practice might go like this: The team was running through the trails in Memorial Park. In the course of the conversation, Ryan brought in an anecdote from the grocery store where he worked. "Geez," Almond said, "do you have any life outside that place?" His teammates ribbed Ryan all the time about his devotion to his job, but somehow when Almond did it, it seemed like evidence of a deep–seated dislike. Whatever Almond's real feelings toward them, Ryan, Matt, and a few of the other boys believed that their coach played favorites against them. Ryan slowed down and ran with Patrick, his best friend.

Mike Overholser broke the silence. "So, Aiman," he started, "do you wanna go up to Boardman tonight?" The social relationships on the team centered on the flamboyant Mike, Aiman, and Isaac. Paul and Matt sat comfortably in this circle of friendship, with Joe looking in. "Do you wanna try to get together with those girls again?"

"Why would you want to do that, Mike?" interrupted Stogus. "You don't like girls." Stogus and Mike had recently begun a verbal feud. The boys got tired of the way Stogus antagonized people, but they respected him for standing up to Mike, who was no pacifist.

"Stogus," Mike came back, "that's like the millionth time you've said that. Nobody's laughing." As those two continued their insults, Ryan, Patrick, Josh Matthews and Tommy Yuhaniak ran together in a quieter group. Jason Stewart, Erik Cibula, and Lance Murphy traveled freely between the two main groups. The Quakers were willing to make great sacrifices for their team, but not necessarily for all of their teammates. On some days they could hardly stand each other.

Joe had again fallen into his annual slump, and Almond was too good a coach to ignore it this year. He had caught on to the pattern of Joe's cross country seasons: a strong summer, one or two good early races, midseason stagnation, and a moderate improvement near November. That contrasted both with Almond's plan and with the other Salem runners. Many of the boys, like Ryan last year, improved incrementally throughout the year. Others, like Paul, stalled halfway into the fall, but ended the year with significant PR's. A few did sputter out like Joe, for one reason or another. But none of them faltered for three consecutive years in the same predictable way.

Almond and Wilson conferred and decided that Joe's problem stemmed from an inability to recover quickly from hard workouts. Wilson, when he was an All–American at Malone College, had dealt with the same setback by taking extra rest days. Almond called Joe into his classroom one day and presented an individualized training plan. This was not the first time the coach had tailored his program to a single runner; last year he had cut Aiman's running to accommodate his soccer schedule. Almond stressed his flexibility and hopefulness. "If you cut back to one hard workout a week," he promised, "I'm sure you'll start feeling fresh."

"Coach, what if I'm just mentally weak?" Joe wanted to think that all his running difficulties were physical. But he struggled to believe it.

"No one thinks you're a head case," Almond insisted. Joe decided to drop the point and listen to his coach. Running more slowly to achieve faster results seemed counterintuitive and cowardly, but Joe would try nearly anything to get himself out of this slump. That afternoon Joe ran at "medium" pace and cheered for his teammates as they ran a workout through heavy rain at Centennial Park. The torrential downpours were remnants of a storm that had made its way up from Florida into the heart of the Midwest. The runners nicknamed the run "The Hurricane," apt because of both the rain and the tight spin they took around the park loop.

The workout consisted of ten, 600m repeats. Even without the mud, it would have been one of the hardest days of Salem's regimen. The runners knew they would be winded after one 600, exhausted after four, and ready to pass out after seven. "Now, don't kill yourselves trying to hit your goal times in this mess," Almond had prefaced today's practice. "Just keep your effort hard." Some kids might have used the coach's disclaimer as an excuse to take it easy, but Almond knew his boys would try as hard as ever today. Some of them might try even harder.

After the warm–up, Coach Wilson pulled Patrick Gorby aside and spoke quietly to him for several minutes. Gorby was running faster than most people could ever hope, but no one – including Gorby – thought he was fulfilling his potential. Whatever the boy's mental block, Wilson's pep talk dissolved it. Gorby sprinted through the first six hundred, leaving his teammates to wonder what exactly Wilson had said. The skinny sophomore kept it up, too; he set his face in a glare and burned through repeat after repeat. Aiman let his teammate lead. The cocky soccer player did not care about winning workouts as long as he could win races. Paul, however, cared very much about beating his teammates in training: he knew that was the only way he could improve relative to them. Isaac ran among them, now ahead and now behind, and Mike Overholser hung onto the leaders for a few loops of the 600m course. With this competitive dynamic, and in these mucky conditions, the boys did not reach their goal times: they shattered them. After the tenth repeat the team slid around in the mud, rewarding themselves with mindless fun. It felt good to be fast.

Wednesday's workout was not the only thing to boost the Quakers' confidence. Wednesday night saw the release of the State Cross Country rankings, and Salem topped the Division II list. "Where's Edgewood now?" Paul asked at Thursday's practice. He found vindication in the number-one rank. After going through all last year ignored by the running community (until the end, when they were condemned by it), the Salem boys had won respect. He, Mike, and Yanek dissected the honor before practice began, discussing the process by which coaches voted in the rankings and how many teams Salem had beaten.

Aiman disliked the stock his teammates were putting in strangers' opinions. They had not cared about the rankings last year; why should anything change? "We already won State, guys!" he shouted with mock–adulation.

"Don't get overconfident," cut in Almond, missing Aiman's irony. "Those rankings don't mean much. Personally, I'd rather we not have the pressure of being ranked. Just try to shrug it off. Say, 'Well, guess we couldn't stay under the radar.'" His runners did not mind the attention. And now that they had been detected, they resolved to be more than a blip.

Their times in the first two official meets convinced the Quakers that they were good. And not just "State Championship" good; Salem's boys began wondering if they were not the best team in Ohio, regardless of division. Division II traditionally produced weaker teams than D I, with its massive enrollments, and D III, with small schools like

Maplewood and McDonald that focused entirely on cross country instead of splitting their athletes among soccer and football. Salem had yet to see how they would compare with competitive teams since their first two meets had drawn only local schools.

Fortunately, Salem's next race was at the Tiffin Carnival, 150 miles west in Tiffin, Ohio. The meet sprawled across acres of park and drew the best teams from every division in Ohio, and even out–of–state powerhouses looking for competition. "I'm entering you guys in the D I race for two reasons," Almond told his team before the race. "First, we don't want D II teams to see how they stack up against us until Regionals." To this end, Almond had convinced the X–tra Mile Club to buy seven new uniforms for the varsity runners. Instead of a conspicuous SALEM across the chest, they read, cryptically, SCC HARRIERS in small letters. Hopefully, no D II coaches would notice the boys. "The other reason is to face the best competition, because blowing teams out in a smaller race isn't going to help us do better at State."

Saturday afternoon found the Quakers stepping off the spacious bus that the X–tra Mile Club had chartered for the three–hour journey. The sun blazed onto picnic tables, lemonade stands, port–a–johns, vendors hawking funnel cakes, and row after row of tents full of runners. Races were run throughout the day, so all of the kids were in different stages of preparation or celebration. Some lazed, some focused, some warmed up, some cooled down, some stretched, some ate, and some threw Frisbees (the mark of a team that did not take itself seriously, Almond had said). Then there were the boys and girls who actually raced, weaving through the sea of spectators and competitors that saturated the otherwise dry grass.

One of Almond's coaching friends let the Quakers use his team's tent. The runners spread their gear and their bodies under a nearby tree, where they could wait for their races to begin. Almond's contact had picked out a prime spot – there was a high demand for shade on days like this, when the sun seemed to suck the life from anyone exposed to it. It roasted the boys as they walked the course, and the Quakers found themselves awaiting the next patch of shade along the route. They usually raced in the morning, before the air could ignite at noon. Joe gulped bottles of water, but the moisture seemed to evaporate instantly from his skin.

Joe's body felt the way it usually did before a race: his legs dragged and his nerves tingled. But he knew that Almond had removed any chance that his recent slump was physical. If he did not show up with a great performance today, he would have no excuse. The race was going to be hot for everyone.

"This is the fastest course in the State, boys. It's a downhill sprint with good competition," Almond declared. Paul was excited about the whole situation. Fast course, good competition; his team would make some noise across the state, and everyone would come home with a nice PR. The only thing that stood in the way of a new time to brag about was the extreme heat that filled the air. The temperature reached 75 degrees, with the sun–soaked ground radiating heat. With hours until their race, the top seven Quakers made conscious efforts to avoid the sun.

The girls and the JV boys ran first, so the varsity boys could spend the hours watching those races. At meets like Tiffin, where dozens of teams entered a single race, "open" races were scheduled for junior varsity runners and teams of fewer than five. These races allowed eighth and ninth men from top teams to dominate in a way that they normally could not. For example, Yanek and Josh finished among the top third of the open race, though they would have finished minutes behind the leaders of the DI race. Stogus shaved thirty seconds from his previous best, Tommy returned from an injury with a decent time, Lance slogged through a head cold, Jason PR'd, and Erik faltered after a huge improvement last week.

The string of personal bests surprised no one: Almond had prepared his runners for the fastest course they would see all year. Runners blazed such fast times at Tiffin, in fact, Almond said that the Quakers might not run faster all year – even at the speedy Scioto Downs when they were in peak shape. The boys saw their teammates' improvements and hungered to race.

Because of the heat, they spent even less time on their warm–up than they had last week at Marlington. After ten minutes of trotting around in the sun, the boys dripped with sweat. Joe drenched himself with water before he jogged to the starting line, and convinced Mike and Aiman to do the same. By the time the gun fired, the droplets had already stopped running down his chest.

Things went wrong quickly. Patrick, Aiman, and Isaac, who usually put themselves within striking distance of the race's leader early in the race, realized that their normal speed placed them in the middle of a race with so many fast DI runners. Aiman and Patrick had run at State last year, but there had not been such a strong field even there. If they had started out faster they might have latched onto the lead pack and hung on until the finish, but as it was the Quakers remained behind while the frontrunners broke away.

Paul opened the first mile unspectacularly. He used the first half–mile to get a feel for the race and then began moving up in the field. He caught Isaac and immediately set out to break him. Isaac hung on, and together they reached Patrick Gorby. The three Quakers did not stick together for long, however. Gorby fell back, and Paul broke away from Isaac soon after. By the second mile, the team was completely broken up into seven individuals. Until the Salem boys learned to run together, to push each other to faster times than any of them could reach on their own, they could not be a "great" cross country team.

Joe had started his race with no concrete goals, only a general hopefulness. His hopes were rewarded when he caught sight of Mike near the mile mark. He kept the Salem boy in his focus and let his legs reach infinitesimally farther on each stride. Overholser would be his. Meanwhile Ryan, without Josh there to pace him, ran without the drive that had powered him during his steady improvement last season.

The race ended without celebration. Salem as a team had placed ninth, humbling the boys. Given the way they had finished at Tiffin, a State Championship was by no means a given. Aiman continued his pattern of leading the team, with Paul close behind. Isaac, now beginning to plateau, repeated his time from Marlington. Gorby followed him, and Mike rounded out the top five. Only Aiman had run a P.R., and Ryan Griffith had raced especially poorly without Josh Matthews in the race to pace him. Matt Yanek, running in the open race, had finished with a faster time. For Yanek, who was finally making up the ground he had lost in the summer, it was an important stride toward the varsity spot he sought so fervently.

The runner with a true breakout race was Joe, who ran 17:42 and nearly beaten Mike. Apparently Almond's tweak to the training program had worked, and he wanted to make one more modification. During the week after Tiffin the coach changed Joe's workout day from Monday to Wednesday, a difference he insisted was immaterial. But Joe suspected that Almond's latest shift was actually detrimental, and that was only one of the running demons Joe allowed to plague him. If he ran a workout too slowly, he cursed himself for giving in to fatigue. If he ran better later in the week, then that was only because he had not worked hard earlier. He slept too little, he ate too much, he ran too little on long days, he ate too little, he worried too much, he ran too hard on easy days, he relaxed too much, he ran too slow on hard days, he asked Almond too many questions, he smiled less and less. The more he day–dreamed about Cross Country (sitting in class, standing at play practice, marching during halftime of football games), the less appealing the actual running became.

For the rest of the year, Joe did not have another race like Tiffin. Ryan beat him again at Malone College, Almond and Wilson's alma mater, Columbiana, where Salem easily won the County Championship, and the Cuyahoga Valley National Park, the hilliest course any of the runners had ever seen. Notwithstanding Joe's difficulties, these midseason meets helped build the Quakers' confidence as the postseason neared.

Starting at 6:45 AM on October 9th, boys and girls began arriving at Salem's Memorial Park for the Metro Athletic Conference Championship Meet. Salem High School was one of the smaller schools in the MAC, but the Salem boys knew they would dominate the meet, possibly taking the first four spots in the race. There were a few talented individuals in the race, but Almond put little pressure on the top boys to perform well in a race whose outcome did not really matter. It was more of an opportunity for several of the runners to regain confidence, including Patrick and Paul, who had been in a slump for some time. Also, as the penultimate meet in the regular season, the MAC championship would heavily affect Almond's decision about who would run varsity in the tournaments.

Almond had re–designed Salem's course last year, and the current route through Memorial Park included a 180-degree turn and a steeplechase–style leap across a small creek. The course record was just over 17 minutes, but a beautiful day and a dry course made it likely that the record would fall. After racing through extreme heat in some meets and a torrential downpour in another, the Quakers had finally gotten sunless, windless, rainless, perfect conditions.

The race started out at a quick pace, and as usual Paul wanted no part of it. He was barely in the top 7 on his team at the 800m mark, when he opened up and continued to the front of the pack. The front was relatively crowded, considering how little competition the Salem team had expected. Aiman and Patrick filled two of the top spots and Paul joined them shortly after crossing the mile marker. The lead runner made a break as the course headed toward the woods, and it became clear that he would not be caught after the pack lost line of sight of him in the forest. He would eventually won the race with a course record in the low sixteens. Patrick made a similar move on Paul and Aiman, who continued to work together moving through the field.

For Joe, the gun did not bring the usual shift into race mode. He felt tired after 800 meters, and he fell behind people who had not been close to him throughout the season: Tommy Yuhaniak, Stogus, and Lance Murphy. Matt Yanek and Josh Matthews were out of sight, racing each other for the seventh spot on the team. Joe was in twelfth.

Well, he mused, *I guess I'm off varsity. I'll probably look back on this as one of the worst days of my life.* His pace felt terribly slow, but somehow he could not go faster.

Paul finally broke Aiman as they exited the woods and made their way to the final 800m. Gorby had built a large enough gap that Paul had no chance of catching him, but still had to worry about several runners chasing him. The Quakers ended up with disappointing 2nd and 4th place finishes, followed by Isaac and Aiman together in 7th and 8th. The only impressive aspect of the team's race was their top five's average time: 16:50, the best in Division II by over 15 seconds.

"Shouldn't have played soccer all week, you could've won the thing," lectured Almond, again trying to convince Aiman to quit his other sport.

As the boys congratulated and debriefed their teammates, Paul realized that his cousin had run a terrible race and placed twelfth for Salem. He saw Joe and approached him. "What happened?" Joe shook his head. He had no good explanation for a poor race when nearly everyone else on the team had set a P.R. He wanted to evaporate into the cool fall air, but instead he floated around the course aimlessly.

"Joseph!" Paul's father, Joe's Uncle Paul, called to him. Uncle Paul, a dentist, had a theory about Joe's sub–par performance. Last Friday, an oral surgeon had given Joe an apicoectomy, a procedure that had involve removing infected tissue from Joe's jawbone and filling the space with a bovine bone graft. The day after the surgery Joe had raced without impediment at Cuyahoga Valley National Park, but his uncle explained that sometimes the body takes a week to respond to stress. "So, don't worry about today's race," he concluded. "Just get some rest, and by next Saturday you'll be fine."

So Joe rested. After crying for awhile at home, he took a nap. He did not run at all on Sunday, and on Monday he ran at a moderate pace while his teammates jetted around the track. Before Monday's practice Almond talked to him. First he checked off the tangible factors: "You're getting enough recovery, your diet is good, and your blood lactate level is normal." Then for the tricky part: "You need to be having fun. Are you having fun?"

"Uh…" *No. This sport is making me miserable, and every bad workout I run is making me feel worse and worse about myself.*

"Don't answer that. Just remember that you've gotta take pressure *off* yourself." Joe agreed to try, and the conversation shifted to lighter topics as the pair jogged from the High School to Reilly track.

The pressure resumed shortly thereafter. The next day Joe's dad talked to Almond on the phone about the apicoectomy, and told his son that Almond would give him the varsity spot if he ran well this weekend. Wednesday was the PSAT. Thursday Almond held a meeting in his room; the primary subject was earning varsity.

"I'll be putting a lot of stock in Saturday's meet," he promised. "On hearing that, someone just folded. And that's good; I don't want that person on the team." Joe felt like a participant in a parody of the Last Supper. *Is it I, Coach?*

The varsity was coming off its best team race of the year, and the boys expected to continue improving up to their peak at State. According to Almond's training program, the high volume mileage would now gradually decline and the focus of training would become intensity. Speed work at the track began the week before the Sim Earich Invitational, but mileage did not drop. This worried Paul; his coach's program had never let him down when he followed it, but too much of a good thing (like high mileage late in the season) can ruin a runner. Paul pushed the fears aside and prepared for the meet; it was his time to take the reins of the team again, and this time not let go of them.

The final regular season meet was the Sim Earich Invitational. It was hosted at the Trumbull Country fairgrounds, the same location as the following week's District Championships. The meet was a feel–good tune–up for the postseason; it had decent competition, an unbelievably fast course, and it excited the team about the subsequent weeks and eventually the State meet. A new challenger to Salem would also make an appearance at the meet: Walsh Jesuit.

Walsh was a Catholic school in Cuyahoga Falls, near Akron, and it drew elite runners from a number of nearby school districts. The Warriors had missed qualifying for State in 2003, but only because their lead runner had collapsed during the Boardman Regional meet. Salem had heard talk of them all year, but really became interested when the team posted a sub–17 top–five average the same day Salem had. Neither team had a noteworthy front runner; both relied on pack running and teamwork. Despite the pressure, Salem looked forward to taking on Walsh before Regionals, planning to beat the Warriors so badly that their confidence would be non–existent during the races that mattered.

On the other side of the spectrum, there was still a varsity and alternate spot open for the JV runners to shoot for. In contention were Matt Yanek, Josh Matthews, Justin "Stogus" Roberts, and Joe, and Sim Earich would be the last piece of information Almond would use to choose the remaining spots.

Since Aiman had raced tired at MAC, Almond advised him to open his race conservatively. "Aiman, since coach wants you start off slow, run the first mile with me and then see how you feel. Maybe you'll like my strategy," Paul told Aiman. When Paul had offered similar advice to Mike last year at Regionals, the inexperienced runner had run a sub–par race. Running an evenly paced race is never easy; one must start in the middle of the pack and gradually work his way to the lead. If he executes the strategy correctly, a runner will almost certainly run a PR, because an even pace is the most efficient. But oftentimes a runner becomes discouraged and his slow first mile becomes an even slower second mile. Aiman had now run cross country for nearly three years, and Paul trusted him to hold steady for the full 5k.

When the race started, the two fell back relatively far from lead. Isaac and Patrick quickly moved to the front and set the pace for the lead pack. The course conditions were horrendous. Mud filled the paths and violent winds blew unimpeded across the open fairgrounds. The runners did not realize how much the conditions were affecting their races until the mile, where a large digital clock displayed mediocre times. By now Paul and Aiman had bridged the gap between Isaac and Patrick, and the four of them fell into stride for the first time all season.

As those four teammates banded together, Yanek, Josh, Stogus,and Joe were battling for varsity. Joe was losing. He had started too slowly and gotten boxed in by the crowd of competitors. By the time he had entered the barn, Griffith and Yanek were far ahead. Joe fought the wind that pressed him backwards, and after a mile he passed Gebs. That meant he was closer to Ryan and Yanek. It also meant Josh had no hope of making varsity. Joe tried not to feel guilty, but Josh had been far from Matt and Ryan as it was. Joe began to doubt that he himself could catch his teammates, and eventually he decided that he could not. He may have been physically capable, but his own assessment doomed him. Yanek and Griffith, running in tandem the way Almond had taught, drew further and further away. The two boys were pulling each other toward great races; they had realized the advantages of running together.

Ahead of them, their teammates continued their assault on the front pack. As the four Quakers neared the start of the second and final lap, they saw Almond and Wilson standing several feet off the course. "Neigh–eigh–eigh–h–h–h!" Wilson let out his trademark horse impersonation, sending chills through the four. He had whinnied like that during workouts throughout the seaoson, and to the Quakers it was almost a subliminal command to run faster. "Horses don't care about fatigue," Wilson had said one day. "Horses care about winning."

There were two breakaway runners that were too far ahead to catch, but the chase pack was only slightly in front of the Salem runners. Aiman attempted to build a lead over the chase pack with about 200m to go in the second mile. He looked back and noticed runners "drafting" him, following behind his shoulder so he would protect them from the wind. Aiman certainly did not want to do the work for opponents, so he began zig–zagging. Paul almost laughed out loud at Aiman's antics.

The top four went through the two–mile mark together, all of them in the top 10 of the race. Pain was setting in for Paul, and he contemplated slowing the blistering pace. There was a whole mile to go, and Paul was sandwiched between some of the top runners in the state. The only force holding him in the front pack was his three teammates, and he knew he was carrying them as well. Running with teammates provided mutual benefits, as none of the competitive Salem runners wanted to lose to another. Together the Quakers moved into fifth through eighth place, and with 1000m to go Paul broke away from his team and began an extended burst to the finish. *Just like last year at Districts, I'm starting to peak now, this is my course* Paul thought to himself. No one would beat him mentally in the last 1k of this race. Paul was firing on all cylinders; his race had been perfect. He moved as far up as 3rd place, but it was impossible to make up ground on the top two. He could only hold his position, and even that would not be easy. He knew he could not slow down at all or he might risk being caught by the pack again and losing to them in the final sprint to the finish line. One runner did manage to pass him, but Paul maintained his pace to the final straight.

Paul began his sprint around the last turn and up the dirt track to the finish. He watched as the boy ahead of him took third place, and he figured he was a lock for fourth. Just as he stretched his final stride towards the finish line, Paul was passed by a St. V's runner that had gained an incredible amount of ground on him in the last stretch. Seconds later, Aiman and Isaac literally crashed into Paul to claim the sixth and seventh spots of the race. Paul was surprised that his devastating late race move was not enough to build a larger gap between him and his teammates. Gorby was next across the line in 9th, and the disappointment already showed on his exhausted face. He had gone from leading the Quakers to a MAC victory to fourth on the team (albeit by mere seconds) in one week. The race proved two things: Almond's program worked, and any one of the top four could be Salem's first runner in any given race. Mike capped off an impressive team finish with a 19th place; the Quakers scored just 46 points.

Paul had accomplished what he had come to do: lead his team into the post–season with a dominating performance against some of the State's best runners. Unfortunately for the runners, the course prevented any fantastic times, and the top four all finished in the 17:10s. That was 50 seconds off Paul's personal best, but certainly one of his best races ever. The team as a whole was excited about their race; never before had they benefited so much from pack running, and never before had the top four run so close together for the second half of a race. Despite the inevitable resentment of losing to teammates that Aiman, Isaac, and especially Patrick felt, the team's morale was at an all–time high.

At this point, Almond had to decide who would make the varsity team between Matt and Joe. He called his top 6 runners over for their input. Paul felt a serious conflict of interest; he obviously wanted his cousin to race with him at the State Meet again, and his arguments would be biased. "Doesn't Joe have the fastest season P.R?" he asked. Almond loved to break ties by comparing personal records, especially for runners on the bubble for varsity – the runner with the faster P.R. would be a better replacement if one of the top five runners got hurt.

"Yeah," acknowledged Aiman, "but that was early in the season. Joe hasn't really improved at all during the year. I think he's got too much on his plate." This was in reference to the fall play, in which Joe had the lead role. From now until State, rehearsals were going to become only more frequent, and none of the runners wanted their teammates to be lessening their commitment to Cross Country. "Yanek's been improving throughout the year; I think you've gotta go with him." The other boys nodded in agreement. Yanek was the better choice.

"All right," said Almond. Paul got the sense that the coach had already made his decision, and was using the boys only to reassure himself. "I'm gonna go with Yanek. But he'd better not fold under the pressure." Almond did not want a repeat of Yanek's performance at State last year; he had to be able to count on each of the top seven. "If he runs bad at Districts, he'll be the alternate."

Watching these proceedings from a hundred yards away, Joe knew what the team's decision had been before Almond walked up and told him. Joe's season, by and large a melancholy one for him, had sounded its death rattle. Now began the postseason, which his teammates would spend vying for a State title and he would spend second–guessing every decision he had made for five months. Joe knew that the Quakers did not need him to win a State title. If (though Joe was sure it was actually "when") the boys did earn a gold at Scioto Downs, Joe would lay no claim to it. He would not allow himself to enjoy a victory of which he had failed to be a part.

And the Quakers looked virtually sure to take first at State. Walsh, their major competition, backed down from the pre– Regional challenge and ran in an open race later that day. They posted average times and would have had no chance against Salem's one-two-three-four combo in the Division II Varsity race. Barring an untimely injury, the only thing preventing the Quakers from winning the State Title was themselves.

Chapter 7

The Challengers

"One who is overly proud will certainly meet defeat."

–Chinese proverb

"We're gonna go to Regionals and win that…then we're gonna go to State and win that too."

A reporter jotted down Aiman Scullion's prediction. It was customary for local sportswriters to interview teams' top runners at championship meets, and at the 2004 District Championships Aiman had led both the team and the race. He felt too enthusiastic to wear his usual mask of modesty, and he seized the opportunity to announce that Salem would win a State Championship. The boys believed that the media – whether or not intentionally – often misinterpreted their comments to make them seem more arrogant, and tomorrow's write–up was sure to portray the Quakers as especially cocky. After giving several reporters comments on his own race, his team's race, and a series of other running–related questions, he rejoined his teammates to review the victory.

"400 meters into the race my legs felt like there was only 400 meters to go; I was just flat the whole time," Paul told his coach, whose positive attitude was confusing Paul.

At Sim Earich the week before, he had been completely focused on the race. He had thought about every stride, and calculated how he could gain an advantage by drafting, or by dodging a stretch of mud by stepping off the course. The spectators had been non–existent to him; they could not move

---

his legs faster so they were not important. At all times he had looked for opportunities to climb up higher on the leader board. But this week was different. "I mean, how do I go from finishing third at this meet last year to eighth this year, one week after the best race of my life? At least I have my bad race out of the way....now I can run great at Regionals and State." Paul's 17:22 was only several seconds slower than the previous week, but conditions had improved somewhat. Regardless, a time starting with "17" was not what Paul wanted this late in the season.

"Guys, don't worry about it," recommended Almond. "I expected you to be flat today. We just got off a great week of training." Interval training had been moved from the winding park paths to the fast track at Reilly Stadium. The goal times had dropped several seconds, but the runners had not stopped there. The track allowed for incredibly fast times, with some members of the team averaging five seconds under their goal times in a 600m. Although Almond encouraged the Quakers to stick to the times he had prescribed, he brimmed with excitement at the splits the team was turning. The only problem with their ultra–fast training was that their legs had gotten tired. Theoretically, the boys would be accustomed to the faster pace by the week of State.

"Now change your attitude and worry about Regionals," Almond ordered his disappointed team. "This race was just a warm–up; don't lose your focus on the goal. We're going to drop mileage again and go into Regionals in the best shape we've ever been in." The training program was not a mystery to them, but they still hated to run slowly. Despite knowing they would be flat today, they had still believed they could pull out a good race.

Aiman succeeded; he overcame the mud and wind to post a 16:46. Patrick and Isaac followed in fifth and sixth place respectively. Although only a single place separated them, Isaac had had no chance of catching Patrick, who was looking stronger every week. They ran 17:01 and 17:12; neither of them was proud of his individual performance. Nevertheless, four runners into the scoring, Salem showed no real weaknesses. How could a team with four runners in the top ten at a competitive District Meet be beaten at Regionals or State? The answer came nearly a minute after Patrick, when the Quakers' fifth runner, Mike, crossed in 17:55. Mike failed to beat the fourth runner from Cardinal Mooney, a team that had little chance of even making it to State this year. Mike claimed 21st place, but that translated to a Regional meet finish in the 70s or 80s and an even worse State finish. Ryan Griffith nearly beat Mike, running an 18:02. The gap between the two of them was normally counted in the tens of seconds. Now it was down to seven.

Almond had been reluctant to give Yanek the seventh spot, because he felt that the senior had folded under pressure at State last year. Matt struggled out with his emotions than anyone else on the team, and everyone could tell how good a race or workout he would have by the way he talked beforehand. If he whined about his parents' yelling at him, or his teammates' running ahead of the main pack on a warm–up jog, or Almond's picking on him over something insignificant, then he was sure to run slowly. But if he smiled and soliloquized about how good his legs felt and how ready he was to race, the Quakers could count on him to deliver. The coach had made it clear that Joe would replace Yanek if the older boy cracked at Districts. Matt, pressured to step up and give the top five runners an added boost through the tournament, finished 32nd in a respectable time of 18:32. Matt had held up under his coach's demands, and he maintained his varsity spot.

Joe was not the sole alternate this year. Although the choice was unusual, Almond decided to reward Josh Matthews for his dedication to the team during his four years at Salem. Almond's choice made sense. The alternate position was already somewhat titular, bestowed more as a reward than in anticipation of some freak accident. Neither Joe nor Josh could really fill in for Aiman if he hurt himself before State. But they could still experience the drive to Columbus, the night–before rituals, and the warm–up at Scioto Downs. Josh deserved that much, at least.

He had been ninth man last year and eighth in 2002. This had been *his year*, and he had tried to make himself a varsity runner and a senior leader. He lacked the speed to be the former, hard as he tried. And he never truly developed into the latter, either. He would occasionally make speeches, but he did not commit to the day–to–day business of building up his teammates. Often his obligations to baby–sit his younger sister forced him to run ahead of the other boys so he could finish and leave early. Other times, like before workouts, he deliberately separated himself from the pack so he could focus. Mike and Aiman would shout variations of their latest catch–phrase, Yanek would tell tales of his out–of–town girlfriends, and Patrick, Ryan, and Tommy would gross each other out with improvised jokes. Maybe they could handle the distractions; Josh needed to focus his mind on running.

Not that his meditations improved his performances all that much: he still finished approximately where he did relative to his teammates in races. And the habit did not endear him to the other boys, either. He came off as aloof, and no amount of joking or conversing at other times could completely erase that image. The Quakers were all supposed to be equals; Almond refused even to acknowledge captains. But Josh did not want to put himself above the other boys, or even apart from them. Paradoxically, he was distancing himself from the team because he wanted so badly to be a part of it.

Of course, all his efforts could not give him any more talent. Four years of sweat, blood, and vomit ended at the Trumbull County Fairgrounds when he finished ninth on the team in the Sim Earich Invitational. He ended his season knowing he had done everything he could to run as fast as possible. Thoughts like that provided him a modicum of solace, and he got over the remainder of the disappointment in the traditional cross country way: with a soda binge. He made peace with the end of cross country just when Almond announced the Monday before Districts that Josh would be second alternate. He appreciated the honor, and the chance to spend the postseason traveling with his teammates. But that proximity was bittersweet. Every second spent at the District Meet watching the race reminded Josh that he had missed his final chance to run varsity for Salem Cross Country.

The more the runners evaluated their Districts races, the better they realized they had performed. Salem scored 37 points in the meet, 20 of which were from Mike. The team's dominance was highlighted by the 51 points the Quakers finished ahead of the second place team, Cardinal Mooney. If Salem's confidence had been strong after Sim Earich, it was now unbreakable. Running flat and tired, the boys annihilated the field to take four of the top ten spots. With Cardinal Mooney behind them, the Quakers were ready for their true test: Walsh Jesuit.

"Our only real competition at Regionals is gonna be Walsh," Almond began practice on Monday, October 25th. "We're the better team, but we could easily lose if we go into the race cocky. They just beat out some good teams to win their District."

"Coach," Paul asked, "didn't Walsh score 89 points at that meet?" 89 points was a score that would win State, when several good teams were in close contention, but Districts? If Walsh scored that many points at Regionals, Salem would win easily.

"Yeah," Almond acknowledged. He liked to be the one giving the team information. "But that doesn't mean they can't beat us. If one of their guys steps up, or if one of our top five tanks it, we could get second at Regionals."

Nothing Almond said fazed the boys, though. Neither did the latest state rankings, in which a few of the twelve participating coaches named Walsh the best team in Division II. The Quakers thought they could not be beaten running in army boots. The entire Region knew that Salem could roll out of bed and qualify for State by finishing in the top six. The Quakers themselves had already begun talk of the State Meet, looking two weeks ahead and ignoring the fact that they could be beaten at Regionals.

Even without Salem and Walsh Jesuit, the Boardman Regional was stacked. Some even considered it a preview of the State

Meet. In 2003, the seven teams from the Region had claimed the top six spots at State (St. Vincent–St. Mary's had finished eighth). Despite qualifying six teams, more than any other Region, the Boardman race would still send some of the best teams in the state home for the off–season. Accepting that Salem and Walsh would have little problem qualifying, the remaining four spots were open to eight teams, six of them State qualifiers from the year before. Hunting Valley University School, Minerva, Aurora, Ashtabula Edgewood, and Mooney all returned talented squads with veteran coaches. The two dark horses were Mogadore Field and Peninsula Woodridge, both having performed well in a talented District. The final spots were likely to be won by a few points or a tie.

The week flew by, as did the workouts. The Quakers were enjoying themselves, running short and fast miles, talking about a State Title.

The day of Regionals arrived, and the boys loaded onto the bus early in the morning. The mood was light; Almond and Mike recited Saturday Night Live skits as the rest of the boys listened. "The one we saw in your room during lunch yesterday was hilarious," Mike Overholser commented. Mike had been skipping lunch to go to Almond's classroom to eat with him. The two would chat about running and watch old Saturday Night Live reruns. In a few short months, Mike Overholser had gone from despising his coach to befriending him.

The last thing they wanted to talk about was the race they planned to win in the next few hours; it was not anything to get worked up about anyway. Whether Almond felt the same way as his team, calm and confident, or whether he wanted to lift some of the pressure off his runners was unclear. It was a side of him that few had seen before, the side he revealed during the season to the runners to whom he felt close. The Quakers descended the bus steps still tossing jokes at each other. Their disputed finish here in 2003 had led to a legal nightmare that marred their season. The ensuing controversy and criticism had left a fire smoldering for an entire year, but the fire was nearly extinguished by their arrogance and pride.

As soon as the Division III race went off, the clouds opened up, bringing sheets of rain down upon the runners. The Quakers scrambled back under their red and black tent and threw water resistant clothes on. The first thing that entered Paul's mind was *Great, we have to run in the rain...slow times, mud, and wet clothes*. Then he realized that every runner had to face the same adversity. But this was Regionals, and a win – whether Paul ran a PR or finished in twenty minutes – was a win.

The negative thought was finally changed into an "advantage" by Almond. "Do you remember last Monday, when we ran an interval workout in 35–degree rain?" he asked the boys. "Everyone went even faster than his goal times. Weather doesn't matter; I don't want to hear about the weather." That workout had shown Almond's fanatical side, his belief that every burden a runner takes on in training is beneficial.

But Almond also had a sensible half. "Now that doesn't mean you should ignore the fact that it's raining," the coach continued. "I want you all to sprint to the front of the race from the gun. With all this mud, it's gonna be practically impossible for anyone to catch the leaders." The advice was meaningless to Paul; he had never run a good race after a fast start, and he did not plan on trying the strategy at Regionals. It was not that he did not listen to his coach; he knew accelerating through the mud was impossible. But he had to choose the lesser of two evils: going out at a good pace and risking never catching the front pack, rather than going out hard and risking spending himself early. His teammates had similar plans. None of them was an outstanding frontrunner, and with a talented field, they could afford to allow other runners to do the work. Salem did not need to be showy.

The Quakers decided to sport their "under–the–radar" uniforms that only varsity runners had been issued. "Everyone will think we're wearing our black jerseys today," Almond explained to his team. "But these white ones, they don't even have 'Salem' across the chest, just 'SCC Harriers.' Coaches, runners, and parents won't recognize us. Since everyone is gunning for us, they're gonna be looking to pass the Salem guys. But if they think you're from some other no good school, they aren't gonna work hard just to get that one point. Those other coaches will be in the dark if they try to score this meet during the race. They won't know how they are doing compared to us. It might also give Walsh a false sense of security if they think no Salem runners are around. Then when the results come out, they'll see that they were tricked." The white jerseys were a significant advantage – not only for the tactical benefits they provided, but also because they made the Quakers even more confident.

As the race drew near, the Quakers sent Josh Matthews out on warm–up sprints in Salem's normal jersey. Everyone would see the red and black and assume the Quakers would be wearing it. But just before the race, Salem's seven racers removed their jackets and wind pants as surreptitiously as possible, so their opponents wouldn't connect the new jerseys to the team they were gunning to beat. They completed several run–outs before stopping out on the soaked course for one last inspirational word by Almond.

"I want you guys to be merciless," he told the boys huddled around him, serious as ever. "You'd better break any team that even gets the idea they can beat Salem. "Let every team here know who is going to win the State Title next week. Break them now, so they are fighting for 2nd in Columbus. Salem on three....but quiet, we don't want anyone to here who we are. One, two, three..." Together they whispered "Salem," and then Almond headed back to his position on the sidelines. The team said a short prayer, and then the Quakers jogged to the starting line for the Regional Championships, the meet that had haunted them for a full year.

"Nothing stupid today, guys," Paul reminded his teammates at the line. "Those officials don't like us and are probably looking to disqualify us. If we lose a runner we might not make it out of this meet, so be careful. No swearing, stay on the course, and don't take your shirts off until you're out of the chute." Obviously officials disqualified runners who cheated by taking shortcuts, and the rule about profanity represented an attempt to enforce good sportsmanship. None of the boys, however, knew why the OHSAA cared so much about what competitors wore and when. All they knew was that athletes could be (and often were) disqualified for wearing jewelry or clothes that did not match.

196 runners looking to put their teams and/or themselves individually in the State meet lined up in the misty rain as the starter raised his blank gun. Muttered prayers could be heard throughout the field just before the pistol exploded, filling the air with smoke. All twenty–four teams broke towards the bottleneck that comprised the first turn, sprinting as fast as they could to avoid being boxed in. By the top of the hill Paul already knew the race was not going well. He felt flat again; his legs were not what they had been two weeks before at Sim Earich. The leaders strung out in the distance, basically unreachable with the mud and wind thwarting any attempt at acceleration. His breathing was noticeably rapid with only a twelfth of the race under his belt, and there was nothing he could do about it.

Meanwhile, the two alternates were standing at the starting line. "Well," said Josh, "Time for our A.T. run." This was the same simple workout they had run last week at Districts: twenty minutes at anaerobic threshold pace. The boys set off, careful to keep their distance from the course and avoid any accusations of pacing their teammates. Joe felt great, and the twenty minute run seemed to last two. It relieved the anxiety he still felt about not making the team, and it made him forget the miserable weather. Unfortunately, his teammates in the actual race did not seem to be doing so well. He and Josh finished their run at the tent as the top seven Quakers were making their way back from the finish chute. The runners seemed grim, so the alternates hesitated. Tommy Yuhaniak, on the other hand, sprinted over to his dour teammates.

"O hey guys, good job!" greeted Tommy.

"Tommy, we ran absolutely terrible, what are you talking about!?" replied Paul, who could not stand people telling him

---

that he or his team had run well after a poor performance. "We got killed by Walsh; everyone ran bad."

"Well," Tommy offered, "at least you qualified for State." That was an achievement worthy of celebration. Why could a JV runner see that, but nobody on varsity could? Tommy wanted nothing more than to be a part of the top seven, so he followed them everywhere. But the top seven wanted nothing more than to be alone at this point, so they tried to drive Tommy off.

"That's great Tommy; now can you leave while we have a meeting?" Aiman said harshly.

"You guys ran faster than I could have," Tommy replied as the team walked away.

"What happened out there, dude?" Paul asked Aiman.

"I got out too slow," Salem's first runner answered. "The rain was terrible and I couldn't make up any ground on the leaders the whole race. Walsh had so many guys ahead of me, I know we lost to them."

"Yeah, I still felt really flat," agreed Paul. "I wonder if I hammered too hard in that workout. The race was just like last year. All these kids that I can beat all year kill me at Regionals. I finally got into the top thirty late in the race, and I saw Gorby and Isaac, but you were out of reach. I just couldn't move in that mud. I did worse than last year: 32nd and a freakin' 18:06."

"I caught up to Aiman at the end of the race," said Gorby. "We both finished in the 17:40's. I think we were 17th and 21st."

"I suck," Mike said, as everyone looked at him. He had just run an 18:44 and finished in 59th place. If he did not get his act together, the Quakers would not be going home State Champions from Columbus.

"Don't worry about it," Yanek said. "I'll bet we won anyway." Ryan nodded. He had run only 19:15, so he could sympathize with all of his teammates. He doubted Yanek's suggestion that the team had won, but any hope was welcome.

"Paul, I thought you would come with me in that last 300m stretch," Isaac said, puzzled at Paul's lack of will to kick at the end of the race.

"I was dead, I had nothing left. Man, Coach is gonna yell at us for three hours after this. I just couldn't go any faster. I wonder how bad we got beat?" said Paul, as the team finally made it back to the tent only to be met by an enraged Almond.

He sat the runners down and chewed them out in front of the tent. "I told you guys to go out hard, and what do you do? You go out slow. A mile into the race, Walsh had their *whole team* ahead of Aiman. And you wonder why we ran badly." Maybe bad tactics had played a role, but Paul wanted to blame his performance on flat legs. He had developed into a fairly consistent mental runner, not allowing pain to get in the way of a solid race. The only hindrance could have been fatigue from his training. Could he have peaked at Sim Earich? Almond denied any responsibility before anyone could question him. "We are peaked, guys. There is no excuse for running the way you did."

The results came in and confirmed the team's predictions: Walsh 108, Salem 116. That's all they looked at. It would not be until later that night they looked to see who else qualified for the State meet. Those other teams meant little to nothing. All that mattered was the fact that they had *lost*. "Could you have made up eight points in the woods? Yes." Almond told the disappointed runners. But as he cooled off, he saw the bright side of the situation. "If we can run that poorly, and only lose by eight to a team that just ran the race of its life, imagine what we can do at the State Meet with a *decent* team race." That rationalization did not satisfy the boys; they had been taught not to lose. No excuses, they had trained for five months to win State *and* Regionals, not just the former. Almond did not seem satisfied either, he struggled to grasp his team's loss. "A freshman finished as Walsh's top runner. We lost every spot to them except the fourth spot. Their number one beat Aiman, number two beat Gorby, and so on. We can't have that." With that said, Almond headed back to the girls, who were nervous as ever.

Paul led his team off to a secluded area in the woods and gathered them in a tight circle. "Guys, we ran like crap. But that's good news. Because if we were that close to Walsh running like that, I guarantee we can beat them by 50 points at the State Meet." 50 was just the first number that popped into Paul's head; he needed an exaggeration to motivate his team and help them forget about their races. Deep down, he did not know if they would win the State Championship anymore. Each of the top five would have to run his best to pull out a first–place finish. Paul also doubted himself after his two poor races in the last two weeks. But he did not let his team know how he felt; he gave them the impression that he was the most confident runner on the planet, and they believed his reassurances.

As the Quakers' moods lightened, the sun came out to warm the girls' race in the afternoon. A second place finish by the guys shook the girls, and caused even more worry. If they ran like the boys had, they would not qualify for State. Almond believed the girls would make it to State, and had attempted to instill confidence in them by reserving their hotel rooms in Columbus for the following week. To take it one step further, he had handed out room assignments on the bus ride up to Boardman. If the girls had any doubts before Saturday, they were gone now.

The boys were stationed on a desolate stretch on the course so that the girls could see their fans and teammates without searching through crowds of people. The girls' field had drastically improved during the last year, and the Salem girls started at the back of the pack. The boys stayed on the same spot after the girls had passed so they could watch them again on the second loop. The second time around was even more alarming, when Deirdre Clary, the seventh place finisher at the 2003 Regional meet, failed to break into the top 15 runners. Liz Shivers, Joe and Paul's freshman cousin, was right behind her. Behind the top two girls was Erin Murphy, who had qualified for State in 2003 as a freshman.

The guys' team sprinted to the finish line about 400m from their spot on the course after the girls had run by for the second time. With what little energy they had left, they managed to arrive just in time to see the first girls finish. Deirdre and Liz finished in the top 25, 20th and 22nd, just enough to qualify for the State meet. Erin came in a minute later in 62nd place. Junior Kimberly Kenst, who was part of the original junior high school team in 2000, finished next in 92nd and was closely followed by freshman Sarah Yerkey, who took 104th place. The boys watched in despair as the girls ran to disappointing finishes, and they wondered if the girls would be fortunate enough to take 6th place. But when the results came back, the Salem girls came up short, by a mere seven points. It was a matter of each of them passing one or two more runners, or not getting out–kicked, or pushing harder when the race became tough. The boys' race took a back seat as the coaches and parents tended to the Quaker girls, who had all broken into tears.

Despite qualifying for State, Liz and Deirdre were as heartbroken as their teammates. They had been a part of a team the whole year, and running as individuals would not be the same. When questioned about the race, Deirdre described her feelings as "bittersweet." The eighth place finish was not one girl's fault, but a slightly sub–par race by each of them. They would have a whole year to think about every little thing they had failed to do during the season: getting to bed early, hitting their workout times, eating right. But now was a time for grieving, as a team, because Salem won and lost together, and Almond had always stressed that point.

The sight was not what Almond had planned. There was no celebration this year, only "ifs" and "could have beens." He tried to console the girls and lift the boys' chins up, but to no avail. Five months of hard work and dedication made Regionals one of the most important days of the year, and failing to do well made each Quaker emotional. They did not dare consider it Coach's fault; the blame fell on the runners because they knew they had the best running program in the state.

Almond did not speak during the bus ride home. In near silence, the boys and girls passed around the results of the races. Almond had conditioned the runners to ask themselves after a loss, "Could I have passed one, two, or five more people in my kick? Did I give everything I had?" The answer was always *yes* to the first question and *no* to the second. Regardless of how fast the girls had run the first 4500 meters, sprinting the next 500 would have been easier than failing to advance from Regionals for the second year in a row. And that last 500 meters would be remembered as easier and easier the more they replayed the race in their minds. They would try to dull that sensation of helplessness by training harder in the winter, spring, and summer. For as many pep talks as he gave, Almond insisted that his runners be able to motivate themselves. The Quakers should be able both to summon and harness an overwhelming desire to make themselves better. There was nothing like a season–ending defeat to catalyze that process.

While the girls grieved, the boys shook their heads. The girls had gone into the race with high expectations, but the boys had departed Salem without considering the possibility of second. In their most optimistic, endorphin–addled moments throughout the season, the girls had given themselves a decent shot at winning State. In their dreariest hours, the boys had allowed for an outside chance of finishing second in Columbus. Now they had taken the silver at Regionals. As they stepped off the bus and mumbled "thank–yous" to the driver, they wondered how it had gone wrong.

Almond walked with the girls to a spot on the grass along the driveway into the parking lot. Wilson gathered the boys around him under the tree where the teams always met. He had said nothing to the Quakers at Boardman. If their defeat had plunged the boys into a metaphorical cave, then the last few hours of contemplation had brought them to its mouth. Wilson was about to pull them into full daylight.

Despite the pair of blows Salem Cross Country had just taken, Wilson did not look at all concerned. He somehow managed to turn any negative situation one–hundred and eighty degrees in the other direction. His positive attitude was undying. Every word inspired his listeners. And although he rarely took a step onto his soap box, everyone gave full attention to him when he did. An athlete can tell when a coach has prepared a speech for motivational purposes. Those speeches become redundant, useless. Coach Wilson never gave one of those speeches; every time he spoke it was spontaneous and heartfelt. He truly believed every word he preached to the runners, and in turn they believed more in themselves. And when Wilson got fired up, the runners got chills from the emotion in his voice. Today the boys were in need of such inspiration, and Coach Wilson was ready to deliver.

His eyes burned as he stood before the boys and began to speak.

"When I left my house this morning, the last thing I said to my wife – and you can ask her – the last thing I told her as I walked out the door, was, 'You just better pray they lose.'

"I'm serious. Why'd I want you guys to lose?" A brief pause yielded no answer to his rhetorical question; the Quakers were intrigued. They runners looked at each other. Why would a coach want his athletes to lose a competition of such importance? Wilson always started slowly. "'Cause losing makes you hungry! I saw you guys sittin' back, sayin' 'This'll be easy; we don't have anything to worry about.' You were sittin' there like a fat dog. And I didn't want you goin' into State like that. So I just hoped somebody would wake you up a little.

"Now that Walsh Jesuit team is sittin' at home with their big gold trophy – that doesn't really mean anything –and they're sayin', 'Oh, that Salem team isn't so tough. We'll beat them next week for sure.' Well, that's stupid. 'Cause every one o' those boys just had the race of his life, and you all crapped down your legs. They don't have any idea how good we really are.

"If you had taken first today, you woulda come back home and yawned and said 'Yep, I guess we're gonna win State.' But in the back o' your mind woulda been a little bit of doubt – you'd be wonderin' if you just might lose. Well, you saw today the only way that's gonna happen. Could any of you have run any worse?" This time a chorus of "no's" answered the orator.

"Now we're gonna see 'em again at State, and they're gonna think they've already won. Pffft. They're done. But we're gonna say, 'You may 'a' beaten us last week, when we all ran with our tails between our legs. But we got a fifty–five gallon barrel o' butt–whuppin', and you can just get in line.'"

The barrel was one of Wilson's favorite devices, and it brought back memories of an earlier speech. The Quakers remembered last year, when the cognoscenti had doubted them. And they got a little bit of that same chip back on their shoulders. *So now they think we didn't deserve all those first place rankings. It doesn't matter what anybody thinks. We know how good we are. And we know we can win State.*

Despite the speech, Paul drove home from the high school that day feeling helpless. State would not come down to him running a great race. It was a matter of how well Walsh ran, and how well Mike Overholser ran. Paul, as well as Patrick, Aiman, and Isaac, would probably not run slowly enough to affect the outcome of the race dramatically. The difference between a good race and a bad race for them was five points. If they all ran decently, Mike would be the deciding factor. He could swing the score by thirty points. The race was not going to come down to a tie like it had so many times in 2003. One team was going to show up, and the other was going to get a whupping. Paul just hoped that his team would choose the former.

Chapter 8

The Promised Land

"Great is the victory, but the friendship of all is greater."

– Emil Zatopek

Almond's words had been ricocheting through Paul's mind all morning. "Guys, I don't know if we *can* win on Saturday. We might just be running for second." Almond had shared this revelation at practice on Monday, and by the end of the week Paul still had not stopped thinking about it. The line was perplexing; Paul didn't know how the words could possibly have fallen from his coach's mouth, especially at such a tense time. Almond kept his intentions veiled. The runners could not decide whether he was trying to keep his team focused on the ultimate goal, or if he had just given up hope after the devastating Regional loss to rival Walsh.

At 8 A.M. on Friday, November 5, the churchgoers from the year before (Paul, Yanek, Mike, and Aiman) with the addition of Joe and Tommy lined a pew at the rear of St. Paul Church in the middle of Salem. Tommy had arrived late, despite actually being a member of the church, which prompted muffled laughter from his comrades. In the silent environment, Paul's mind was swarming with doubts and concerns. Could they have come this far only to place second? Next year was not nearly as promising as the current: Isaac – a quality runner who could fill any spot from one to four – was graduating. If Salem was going to win a State title, it had to be this year, because they might not have another chance for years to come. Even with a solid returning team for the 2005 season, Salem would be hard-pressed to compete with a Walsh team that was constantly recruiting.

Then there were Coach Wilson's thoughts from the same meeting: promising, positive, resolute. "We got a solid top four this year...three of them are going to be in the 16's, and one o' them is gonna have the 'nads' to break 16." The assistant coach had not gained much faith in Overholser, since Wilson was drawn to the selfless attitudes and dedication that Mike simply did not demonstrate. Mike wanted the State title as much as anyone, and often took offense at the coaches' belittling his goals. But Mike did not understand how unenthusiastic he came off at times, joking of quitting and blaming poor races on a lack of motivation. It was another situation where Paul did not know if his coaches were purposely manipulating their runners into being more focused and determined. Mike always resented being the odd man out. The top four had traded spots all year, but Mike remained fifth no matter how well or poorly he performed. Almond took every opportunity to draw attention to the fact, which always irritated Mike. In return, Mike assured his team he would make the incredible 1–2–3–4 punch a complete 1–5 knockout blow.

But after three straight weeks of Mike displaying a deficiency in motivation and an inability to race well under pressure, the Quakers' expectations for their weakest link fell lower and lower. They knew that Mike was the most important part of the team, but given his unreliability, they might have to step up to compensate. Mike guaranteed a career race at the State meet: "I only race well under pressure, and this is the first meet that there has been pressure on me." Paul had seen Mike give up in races throughout the season, coming across the line not nearly as tired as he should have been. Paul shook his head. He would help nobody by worrying about Mike. He just needed to focus on his own race.

After the closing prayer, Paul led Yanek, Aiman, Tommy, and Mike out to his car to drive them to the high school parking lot. "Hey, can we stop at my house to pick up a few CD's?" asked Yanek. They had an hour to kill before the bus was scheduled to depart, so Paul headed over to Matt's house. Matt made the mistake of leaving his disposable camera in Paul's car while he ran inside.

"Hey Paul, do you wanna take some funny pictures with Matt's camera while he's gone?" asked Aiman. Paul immediately grabbed the camera and started capturing useless pictures. When Matt returned, Aiman came clean about what they had done. "Um, we took some pictures while you were gone…."

"As long as there is nothing bad on there, I don't care." Yanek answered, not nearly as angry as Paul and Aiman had expected. "My mom is going to see those, and I don't want to get in trouble." They still had some time left, and Mike badgered Paul into stopping at a local emporium to buy a quartet of ridiculous hats. The five boys finally arrived at the high school just minutes before the bus was set to depart.

"This bus is going to be sweet.," Paul informed his teammates. "My uncle chartered it from some place in Youngstown. I saw some pics of it on their website…it has a TV, stereo system, sink, bathroom, everything you could possibly need." Dr. Mark Shivers, Liz's father and uncle to Paul and Joe, had decided to charter the bus so the kids could enjoy the trip down to State all together and so the coaches would not have to drive for three hours to Columbus. The seats wrapped around the inside of the bus walls, allowing the team to sit and talk for the duration of the trip.

Almond's coaching philosophy revolved around the importance of team. To some, cross country might seem like an individual sport. The team with the five fastest individuals wins; there are no role–players or utility men. An all–star running team should be more successful than one in football or soccer – no interaction is necessary among runners during a race. Theoretically a successful cross country team never even needs to meet, except on the starting line.

Almond did not give that theory a millimole of credence. No one can run to his maximum potential without complete devotion to reaching that potential, and Almond believed that no amount of internal drive could match the motivation created by a group with a common goal. That was why today's American distance runners could not compete with the Kenyans, the Ethiopians, and the Moroccans. The Africans came from a tight group of runners that trained together for the glory of their country; Americans, Almond said, trained for themselves. Almond believed that it was hard to go wrong emulating the greatest runners on Earth. Even his training plan resembled the one used by East and North African national teams.

He often preached about synergism, and how none of the Quakers would be as good without his teammates. The boys fed off each other's energy in workouts and races, and held out their hands for teammates who had fallen behind. In the two–minute intervals between repeat workouts, they encouraged each other and high–fived. They ate lunch together and hung out on Saturday nights. But beyond actions and activities, the boys shared a camaraderie forged over the months and miles. Several were each others' best friends. They sacrificed daily for each other, and – more importantly – the team.

The team trumped any individual. If one of the Quakers raced poorly, but Salem won the meet, then he was still supposed to celebrate. If one of the boys P.R.'d by a minute and his team lost, he suffered the defeat. And if runners qualified for State without their entire team, as Deirdre Clary and Erin Murphy had done last year, they longed for their teammates' company. The pair had been able to share their hopes and anxieties with each other, but not with the girls who had accompanied them throughout the year. Again in 2004, two girls (Deirdre and Liz Shivers) were State–bound without their teammates, none of whom (except for Erin) had ever experienced the State Championships. Deirdre and Liz would do worse if they had to go into the meet by themselves, and the other girls (none of whom were seniors) would do worse next year because they had never been to State before. The solution was obvious: take all the girls along.

Not so obvious beforehand, but noticed by the boys five minutes after the bus left the parking lot, was that the girls placed a much higher priority on their own enjoyment than the boys' peace of mind. The girls giggled and yelled as loudly as they wanted to, regardless of the boys' desire to prepare for tomorrow. The girls had claimed the back of the bus along with the coveted CD player before the bulk of the guys' team had even arrived, straining the runners' already tight nerves.

Even before the bus had left the parking, there were whispers among the guys about the situation. "There is no way the girls should get that CD player," Paul groused to Matt Yanek. "We're the ones who are actually running tomorrow." He raised his voice, "Hey girls, can we put some songs on there?" The girls denied him in unison, and then laughed at their power.

"Coach," Yanek called over the electronic beat, "why do the girls get to sit wherever they want?" It was not as much about the specific problem; Matt could handle three hours of dance music. But he found it unfair in principle, and his acute sense of justice was flaring up.

"Guys," Almond responded, "just be gentlemen. Treat the ladies with some respect." The one thing Almond had never tolerated was immaturity around the girls. May be Deirdre and Liz got some benefit from their teammates' presence, but it could hardly compare to the aggravation afflicting their male counterparts. Paul shut his eyes and waited for the trip to end.

Because there was a chemical toilet in the back, the busdriver did not need to make any bathroom stops. He did, however, pull into the same Wendy's where the team had eaten last year. Almond was creating a rhythm for the dynasty he sought to establish. "Consistency," he often advised, "breeds mental toughness." Yanek and Paul plotted to overthrow the girls by sneaking onto the bus before everyone else finished eating.

The plan was spoiled by Almond, who appeared disgusted that the boys would try to take the back of the bus for themselves.

The guys finally surrendered, resorting to cards and sleep to pass the time. Isaac wrapped his sweatshirt around the hand bar above his seat and pretended to hang himself in protest of the inequality. At one point the girls did throw in one of Mike's punk CD's, but halfway through the first song they removed it in favor of more party music. But the boys were not going to Columbus to party; this was the State meet they had to prepare for mentally. Almond did not seem to take the boys' anxiousness and apprehension into consideration when he refused to force the girls into changing the music. It was just another distraction to obstruct their focus.

The room arrangements were nothing like the previous year. Almond, with his understanding of synergism, had realized that placing the four most rambunctious boys in the same room made next to no sense. He arranged for Joe and Paul to share accommodations with Isaac and Matt. Mike, Patrick, Ryan, and Aiman took the two beds in the other room; Josh would need to bring up a futon or a cot from the front desk. Deirdre and Liz got a room to themselves, and the other four girls (one of them had stayed in Salem) moved their luggage into a room where they planned not to sleep at all. Paul was pleased with the rooms; he could have a good time with Matt, Joe, and Isaac, but would also be able to get plenty of sleep before the big race. Aiman and Mike, always happy with being together, made no complaints about sharing a room with the exuberant duo of Ryan and Patrick. When the bus finally pulled in to the Cross Country Inn parking lot, the team had had more than enough "quality" time together. They went to their designated rooms, changed, and prepared for a run at Scioto Downs.

Paul and Joe's room was adjacent to the girls' room, with only a few feet separating them. "Great," Yanek complained. He was already mad at the girls. "Now they're gonna stay up all night partying, and we won't get to sleep." Paul shrugged it off; he had better things to focus on, and he was a heavy sleeper.

Josh Matthews seemed excited about the prospect of spending the night with the girls' team. Pop, gossip, and late hours would be his consolation prize as alternate, but he would have traded it for a chance to run the next day in a second. Everyone was excited getting off the bus. After fifteen minutes of increasing noise, Wilson called a team meeting for all of the boys available to lecture them on their behavior. Sure it was all right to be excited, but Almond was under a lot of pressure and the guys needed to tone it down a notch. Seriousness swept over the Quakers just as they were preparing to go for a run at the course.

The team piled back into the bus to head over to Scioto Downs, a fifteen minute drive that was extended to thirty when the bus driver got lost. The stadium had not changed at all from last year, only the names and colors on the signs adorning it were different. The boys jogged the course and their memories: "Right over there is where I started to kick." "Here's where I caught you, and then we passed all those guys together." "Remember when Mike peed at the starting line?" It was an opportunity for the boys to reminisce on their past success and begin to get psyched up about tomorrow's race. All of them had been there the previous year, except Isaac who appeared overwhelmed. He had never been under such substantial pressure before. The biggest race he had run was Regionals, just one week before. Now he was being asked to comprise a critical part of a State Championship, to run with poise and confidence against Ohio's most talented runners.

Almond assigned Joe and Josh to measure the course using a GPS watch donated by the X–tra Mile Club. The alternates broke away from their teammates and trotted the full course while the other Quakers stopped after a mile. Almond instructed Joe and Josh to tell only him the course's true distance; the coach did not need his runners worrying about one hundred meters here or there. As it happened, the boys measured the course as a few meters long. Almond took the news without surprise; he believed that the borders of the loops that ran outside the race track were slightly different every year. When Yanek asked Josh and Joe the results of the surveying, the two mumbled that their results had been inaccurate. They felt secretive and important.

After the traditional Spaghetti Warehouse meal of pastas and calamari (Gorby's pre–State race preference), the team made a stop at a grocery store. Almond encouraged the runners to get any snacks needed for the remainder of the stay in Columbus. The school gave the boys' team an allowance for various expenses and the X–tra Mile Club would cover anything over that amount within reason. The girls' team stocked up on soda and energy drinks along with chips and other party foods. Isaac, who consumed only organic food, wanted to purchase a toothbrush. Of course he ran it by his coach, who adamantly refused permission to buy the brush. Almond was not known for his frugality, having tapped into the X–tra Mile Club funds regularly for new jerseys, shirts, and heart–rate monitors. But for some reason he did not want to spend two dollars of the school's money for Isaac's toothbrush. Isaac even offered to borrow toothpaste from a teammate, but still Almond stood his ground. His teammates lent Isaac the money, and yet another minor (though potentially explosive) conflict was resolved.

But Almond was not without plans to lighten the mood of his teams. Naturally, these plans involved Overholser, whose credentials as a jokester were second to none. Coincidentally the act employed the same SNL jokes that the team heard on the way to a disappointing Regional race. Almond gathered the team into his and Coach Wilson's room for their pre–race meeting. "We have a special guest tonight that I invited to talk to you about running and success..." Almond told his anxious runners. Mike, who had gone into the bathroom minutes before the beginning of the meeting, came out. "Hello Monkey Boy," Almond said in a serious tone. Mike walked out in nothing but boxers bandaids on his nipples, and aviator sun glasses, with his hair slicked back. Almond held a hairbrush like a microphone, and pointed it toward Mike as the boy took a vicious bite of an apple. "So Monkey Boy," Almond asked, "to what do you attribute your success as a runner?" Mike replied with a grunt, and then spit pieces of apple in his coach's face. The routine continued with Almond conducting an interview and Mike showering him in fruit. Mike would later say that he did his best to get as much apple on his coach as possible, avenging any past disagreements in a seemingly playful manner. The team tremendously enjoyed the show, laughing the duration. With the pressure lifting and Almond covered in half–chewed fruit, the team dispersed back into their respective rooms for a few hours of sleep before the showdown between them and Walsh.

The Cross Country Inn did not provide complimentary mints on its guests' pillows, it did not contain an indoor pool, and it did not include six–feet–thick, soundproof walls. The lack of the first two comforts made little difference to Paul, Joe, Isaac, and Yanek as they lay down to sleep. But the absence of the third one meant that the four boys could hear the girls next door without straining their ears. They could not distinguish words, but they could easily sense the conversation's ebb and flow. And there were none of the lengthening diminuendos that signal sleep; it sounded as if the ladies were keeping their vow of staying up all night. Accompanying them was Josh, who had decided he would rather share a room with four vivacious girls than with a quartet of sleeping boys. Paul, Isaac, and Yanek offered Joe the option of joining the night–owls, but he insisted on remaining with them. He did not feel like partying while his teammates rested, and he still maintained the hope that he might somehow join them at the line tomorrow morning. So when he walked to the neighboring room it was only to ask its occupants to quiet down. Josh and the girls whispered for a few minutes, and then a roar of laughter brought the volume back to where it had been. Joe's visit was neither the last nor the angriest made by one of the boys that night.

Paul woke up around 8 the next morning to his roommates' complaints about how noisy the girls had been all night. Matt and Isaac were furious; fortunately Paul had slept through the annoyances. They ate the breakfasts they had bought the night before and put their uniforms on under their clothes.

Almond stopped by the room at 9 o' clock and told the team to put on their running shoes; he wanted to get their circulation going and wake them up. They jogged in the cool fall air for about 15 minutes, barely breaking a sweat. The weather was fantastic: 60 degrees, not a cloud in the sky. There was a breeze, but that was not a major concern for the Quakers. The boys went back to their rooms ready to race – but their race was not scheduled until 11:50.

Paul surfed the channels for a movie to keep himself occupied. He found an engaging, nonsensical movie about an oil platform, a giant shark, and treasure–hunting kidnappers. An hour disappeared along with several characters' body parts and, ultimately, the man–eater itself. As the flick wrapped up, the boys from the other room began to stroll over. Patrick Gorby, acoustic guitar around his neck, was the first to enter. The sophomore explained that all four of those runners had slept the night, and that he and Mike had just finished writing a song. Shortly thereafter the lyricist himself entered, and Gorby began playing the guitar. Patrick was still learning the instrument, and his novice strumming usually prompted complaints from his acerbic teammate. Usually Gorby would not be collaborating with Mike anyway; neither was the other's closest friend. But they were teammates, and today they would ride to battle together. Minor annoyances meant nothing today. At State it was possible for Gorby to play rhythm for Mike's free–verse obscenities, and it was possible for them to laugh as though they had been buddies for years. Sports participation creates relationships like that; all those miles make for a lot of common ground.

When Mike ran out of lyrics and the song ended, he spun into a sudden frenzy. He jumped and screamed as though he were at a rock concert. The runners had never seen anyone this wild before a race. The general theory was to save one's self for the demands of running, but it had to take a lot out of Mike to carry on the way he was now. He knew he was the most important runner on his team, and he knew that his race would basically determine Salem's fate. The other Quakers hoped he could maintain this battle rage for the next two hours.

A few minutes after the impromptu concert, the Salem boys and girls gathered all their belongings and loaded them onto the bus. Almond broke the bus ride's silence with a few simple commands. "Don't look at any other teams. They will look at us; ignore their existence. The only team you need to worry about is Salem." Paul knew just about every team in contention at the meet and who their top runners were. He could often name runners as he ran during a race. But Almond wanted the Quakers to look only at each other, because their destiny was in no other team's hands.

At that point, the Quakers still did not know what jerseys they would be wearing for the State championship meet. Their white incognito jerseys had not brought success in past meets, but they were a tactical advantage. The runners expected to wear them, but had both the white and black jerseys in their bags just in case. Almond threw a curveball when he announced that the team would wear the black jerseys. "We want everyone to know who we are." The black jerseys had a giant SALEM on the front that covered most of the jersey. On the back were the runners' numbers and their last names. Paul, like the rest of his team, was excited to conceal his identity no longer. He was a part of Salem, and he wanted everyone in the state to know it.

Soon after arriving at the stadium, Paul caught himself watching other teams. *There's Aurora*, he thought, *but I can't look at them*. He spun his focus back onto his team and rejoined light conversation about the day's race. The boys did not have nearly as much time to lounge as they had last year, a decision Almond had made to prevent the nervousness from boiling over. They walked into the stands to meet their parents, who wished them the best of luck. "Look at this program," Joe's dad pointed out when he saw the boys. "They've got Salem listed as third at State last year." Paul glanced at the page. Sure enough, there was his team in the results, right below Cardinal Mooney. Joe's father seemed vindicated by the black–and–white print. "If this isn't an admission of the team's right to be there, then I don't know what is." Paul's father saw it differently. "It was probably just a typo," he said. "Just not any real attention to detail." Paul did not much care either way. He was finished with last year's controversy, and he wanted no similar experience today. The Quakers would simply have to leave no room for doubt.

They fastened their race numbers to their jerseys, and they made sure their spikes were secure in their shoes.

By then the Division III Boys' race was set to begin, and Almond called his team to transfer their gear to a spot on the racetrack's infield behind a trailer in the shade. All of these preparations were carried out the same way as they had been last year; why try to improve on a system that had worked? The familiar procedures also gave the Quakers a sense of security in the crucial last hour before the race.

There was not a cloud in the sky and the sun beat down hard on the busy course, but the race conditions were still sub–par. A section of the first outer loop had to be closed and a detour added because of mud. The Salem boys ran their warm–up through the first mile from the infield to find exactly what had changed. The wind was also going to hinder the runners with gusts similar to those at Sim Earich three weeks before. But Almond had lectured his team so often about how weather did not matter that the Quakers were numb to it; they would not know the difference between a blizzard and a heat wave. He had also taught them to ignore times and to judge their performances based on place. Today the runners did not care if they failed to break 18 minutes, as long as they walked away with a State Title.

As the start time approached the Quakers jogged over to the line. Most of the other teams had already made their way over and begun pre–race sprints to loosen up. The runners and Almond met at the end of their first sprint for one last motivational speech. He told them to do what they had done all year; that, after all, had gotten them there. The seniors led the group in a prayer before they finally lined up for their run at a State Title. Paul, as he had the year before, said "All–Ohio" to Aiman, except this time he added "first–team" to the end of it. Paul no longer felt under pressure. He was confident and relaxed about his team's ability, and knew that individually his race would come down to his training and not his mentality. It was a matter of whether his legs were tired or not, because he knew he was tough. He hoped to open his first 800 in 2:30, putting himself in good position for a solid sub–5:10 first mile and in contention for a top–10 finish. He trusted his teammates to take care of the rest.

The race started fast, and the Quakers found themselves in the middle of the pack. Paul fell right into his pace while Aiman and Patrick tried to break into the front pack. He discovered that the wind and tall grass made acceleration difficult, which caused the same problem the Quakers had run into the previous week. Despite opening at a conservative pace, Paul crossed the 800m–mark in 2:32, practically perfect. He did not realize though, that the front pack already had 10–12 seconds on him, a gap that was nearly impossible to make up in an elite cross country race. In track he could have run faster lap–splits than his opponents over the course of the race, but in cross country, with a diminished line of sight, hills, and a slower surface, catching the leaders was difficult.

Paul managed to pass Patrick before the completion of mile one, splitting a 5:29. Paul was only five seconds behind Aiman, but the crowd was so dense that he could not see his teammate. Patrick and Mike were both 3 seconds behind Paul, and Isaac went through the mile in 5:37. Neither Griffith nor Matt broke 6 minutes on their first mile, confirming the slow course conditions. Paul was becoming nervous now; he was already out of contention for a top spot and he was running second on his team. He had no idea Mike was so close to him, but he did receive some relief when Isaac caught him early in the second mile. The two made up a few spots in the field before Isaac fell back hard, eventually joining Mike.

Paul re–entered the stadium expecting to feel the same energy surge he had experienced the year before. But when he looked up to the deafening crowd of thousands, he was not affected. As Almond had promised, the second time around a runner is desensitized to the excitement of the race. In most cases, this allows the runner to maintain a greater focus on the actual race and not his surroundings. But without the fans carrying him through to the two–mile mark, Paul struggled. He tried several times to increase his pace, but the attempts seemed futile. He was 10 spots better than the year before at the same point in the race, but instead of moving up, he stalled. He reached the two mile and saw Aiman exiting the stadium not too far ahead. *The same as last year*…Paul thought as he dashed toward his teammate.

By the two–mile mark, Mike had reached Isaac, who was floundering. Mike himself was hurting, but he found the strength to push Isaac. He knew that the meet would come down to the fourth and fifth runners. So, instead of passing Isaac and taking the coveted fourth spot on the team, Mike stayed back with his teammate and shouted encouragement to him. Although the intermittent profanity could have gotten him disqualified, Mike was a better teammate for those last two miles than any Quaker had been all year.

Just as Paul's confidence and optimism peaked, he hit a wall. The wall was both physical and mental; he lacked the energy to catch Aiman and he lacked the will to do it. With 700 meters to go in the race, where he had begun an incredible kick the year before, Paul simply maintained his pace. There was nothing he could do to hasten towards the finish line. When he re–entered the stadium for the second and final time, it appeared that half the field of runners was ahead of him. In reality, there were about 25, similar to the previous year. Patrick caught and passed Paul about 400m from the finish. Paul had nothing with which to counter. Gorby blew by him without any problem and crossed the finish in 16:47, only four seconds faster than the 2003 state meet. Paul came in at 16:54 having lost close to seven seconds to his teammate in the final loop around the track. Aiman had already wandered over to Almond after running a 16:41 and taking the 18th overall spot.

Paul grabbed a cup of water and splashed it onto his face. He convened with his teammates to wait for the remainder of the Quakers to finish. They stood together stunned, as they watched Isaac and Mike stumble across the line mere seconds apart. "How did Mike do that?" Paul marveled. A full minute later Griffith and Matt crossed in 18:11 and 18:13, making no significant impact on the results. "What did you run, Mike?" Paul asked, still unable to believe his teammates performance.

"Low 17's, I don't know exactly," Mike replied softly. He actually had run a 17:15, a giant personal record. Isaac ran a disappointing 17:11, finishing in 42nd place.

"How'd we do, Coach? I didn't see any Walsh guys the whole race," said Paul, still out of breath.

"I don't know," Almond replied. "We ran pretty good, but Walsh stole our trick and wore different jerseys. Did you notice any all–black uni's with a gold W on the chest?"

Paul had expected to know if Salem had won as soon as Mike crossed the line. But since Walsh had copied Salem's strategy of counter-intelligence, he was in the dark until the official results were released. but now he was in the dark until the official results were released. The boys gathered behind the trailer to trade their spikes for training shoes and throw on their warm–ups. The D III results had yet to be announced; apparently there was scoring confusion and the race would have to be tabulated by hand. "Great, more errors," thought Paul as he sat on a pile of pebbles changing his shoes. But the problem did not affect the D II race, and the scoring was completed fairly quickly, just several minutes after the race had finished.

"Today Mike grew a third 'nad," Coach Wilson said to his team as they waited for the results. "So Mike, don't be alarmed when you notice something strange next time you use the bathroom." The humor brought smiles to the boys' faces. Coach Wilson never failed to lighten the moods of the tense Quakers. He did not say anything negative to Isaac about his sub–par race; negative was not in his vocabulary. Whenever he needed to criticize a runner he would preface it with "Now this isn't criticism, it's just a learning experience." And if something remotely unconstructive came from his mouth, one could count on an apology from him. Today he did not even offer mild suggestions; he knew how tense the boys already felt. As he continued complimenting the runners, Almond ran up and announced that the scores were in.

The Quakers rushed over to view the results that had been posted just outside a trailer where the meets were scored. Their eyes went straight to the #1 team spot, which read "Salem 61." They erupted in celebration, screaming and yelling and hugging one another. Still, it was more of a relief they were celebrating than the actual victory. Paul felt like a championship boxer who had just retained his title; he knew the Salem Quakers were the best, and now that they had defeated their challengers he could relax. After the initial jumping and high–fives, Paul reviewed the scores to see who else had done well. He noticed the second–place team, Walsh, had scored 109 points. "Dang it guys, if we had run two places better, my prediction would have been right," Paul joked. Not only did Salem win by an enormous margin of 48 points over a team that had beaten them the week before, but the Quakers' total of 61 was one off the D II State Record for fewest points. With Mike bridging the gap between the top four and himself, Salem placed all five scorers in front of every other team's third runner. The top five averaged 16:58, 15 seconds better than second–place Walsh. The runners ran out into the middle of the infield to signal to their parents and fans that they had won the meet. In reply, an entire section of the stadium went crazy, cheering loudly enough for the runners to hear.

Paul's own excitement about the team's success was giving way to scrutiny about his individual performance. He did not know why his race had been so poor. He did not know why

Aiman and Patrick and Isaac had run sub–par. He blamed the speed work that Almond had thrown at them in the last few weeks, but the coach assured the Quakers that the program was was not at fault. Maybe they had just run the workouts too fast, too far under their target times. But even if they had not raced as well as they had wanted, they had dominated a very talented state meet. Individual performances were not a priority; they had come to win the meet as a team, and that was exactly what they had done.

Joe was saddened as he looked at his celebrating teammates. He had given Josh the pass that would let Salem's alternate onto the course, so Joe had watched the race with all the other spectators. He had initially been happy for his friends, but now his thoughts were turning to self–pity. *If only I had run faster and made varsity*, he thought, I *could be sharing this joy.* As was typical, his mother comforted him. "You're here," she told him, "Try to enjoy it."

So he forced himself to relax as the other boys ran into the stands, and he stood on the outskirts of the customary frenzy of hugs. Maybe he could not fully experience the championship, but he could experience enough of it. The challenges he had faced, his successes and failures, had been worthwhile. Joe smiled.

Now there remained only the true acknowledgement of Salem's victory: the boys prepared to mount the podium. "This is the Promised Land," Almond said to the boys as they strode toward the platform. "Take your shoes off." They obeyed, and stepped barefoot onto the white metal podium.

"And your 2004 Division II State Champions…" blared the loudspeaker, "Salem." Aiman stood on top with Paul and Patrick at either side. He was in athletic nirvana, somewhere soccer could never take him. Whether he would end his soccer career at that point was unsure, but a State Title in cross country was tough to ignore. Although he had not raced as well as he had hoped, Isaac did not pout. Success was based solely on how well the team did. Mike was unusually quiet;

overwhelmed by the situation he had been instrumental in creating. Ryan and Joe stood on the ground, due to the lack of spots on the podium. The Pact had been fulfilled, and Josh and Matt's smiles offered evidence of their jubilation. Since Josh was the second alternate, no medal was available to him, but he did not seem to mind. Almond and Wilson flanked the team wearing Salem hoodies, and remained stoic, barely holding back the excitement they were feeling after their first State Title as coaches.

Pictures were snapped by parents and the official meet photographer. Then Almond ordered them to about–face so one of his friends could take a picture that included the stands in the background. When the boys stepped off and shook the hand of the OHSAA official who had given him their medals, they could see he was seething. "Everybody's mad because we didn't wear shoes," Almond explained quietly, "and because we took that backwards photo." Paul was unsure whether the coach had deliberately intended to snub the OHSAA, but Almond was smiling either way.

Now the rigmarole was over, and the boys dispersed to talk with their families and drink no–longer–forbidden soda. Aiman's mom was assigned the duty of holding onto the trophy, a responsibility she did not take lightly. She adamantly refused to let anyone – team members included – hold the award, despite their part in earning the trophy.

As Paul followed Deirdre and Liz's race around the 5k course, he thought again about his performance. It was a habit never to be content, to tear his race apart piece by piece and find out what he had done wrong. He had not achieved All–Ohio status, he had placed 3rd on his team, and he had not helped his teammates run better. But the truth of the matter was that he had just won a State title. Salem could not have done it without him, just as they could not have done it without any member of the team. Take Isaac out, and Salem would have lost by seven points. The Quakers may have won by a significant amount, but without each piece of the puzzle it would not have been possible.

Almond and Wilson had put that puzzle together. In three years they had turned the Quakers from county contenders into State Champions. During that time they had endured doubts about their coaching philosophies. They had sacrificed hours of their time for a handful of high school runners. They had never known how a race, much less a season, would end. Today, though, Paul thought the victory almost seemed like fate. He realized how unlikely it was for a position to open up at Salem the very year Almond was searching for his first head–coaching gig. Watching his coaches and teammates, he marveled at the way this group of runners had come together. Mike had moved from Minerva, Ohio, in elementary school, and only joined the team because he was bored one summer. Almond had literally gone to his house at times to convince him to stay on the team. Aiman had lived in Morocco till fourth grade, and just happened to return to his dad's home town of Salem. Josh Matthews had moved to Salem from North Carolina in fourth grade. Patrick had started running in 7th grade after the junior high track coach recommended the sport to him. Matt Yanek was a football player until junior high, when he had decided to roll the dice on another sport. Paul did not even know why Ryan had joined the team his sophomore year; he had just shown up one day and decided to be a runner, with no previous knowledge of the sport. Then there was Isaac, who had barely made the deadline for transferring to Salem. His school's superintendent had almost not released Isaac to leave.

The only constants over the years were Joe and Paul, who would have run regardless of success and glory. Together they had witnessed the unthinkable. In just three years, Salem had gone from a fifth place District finish, to a half–State appearance, to the Division II State Champions. If Almond had shared his ambition to bring a State Title to Salem in such a short time period, most would have laughed at his naive dream. But a dream is not a dream unless people think it is impossible. Paul was not one of those doubters. His goal had been a State title since he had known the meet existed. He had not known what it would take to be the best, how a talented enough team could be assembled, or the difficulty of improving so greatly in just three years. He had just known it would happen.

A friend had once told Paul about his own days in high school athletics. He had won an individual State Championship in track, only to find several hours later just how little most people cared about that victory. Paul now knew what his friend meant. The masses would forget Salem's title shortly; it would be just another line in a record book. But the difference between Paul and his friend was that Paul was not alone in his triumph. He had his team to celebrate with, to remember every last moment of their State championship year. He was a part of something greater than he could possibly have created alone.

He continued musing as the team packed up and walked back to the bus, as the boys and girls stopped at a restaurant on the way back, and as they rode home trying to convince themselves they were not dreaming. He thought about the days and years ahead. The name Paul Shivers might not be remembered even by citizens of Salem, but his team would go down into school history forever. And he would be able to look back and say "I was on that team. We were the best." Standing a step lower than Patrick and Aiman on the podium did not matter. When the administration hung the championship picture in Salem's lobby, the students would not look to see who placed where. They would glance and see "Salem 2004 State Champions." It did not matter that Paul had not finished as an All–Ohio runner. He had helped achieve the team's goal, and that, finally was enough.

Epilogue

Hours after Salem's winning the 2004 State Championship, Mike Almond's life began a series of dramatic changes. While the team was stopped at a restaurant on the way back to Salem, Almond received a call that his infant son had started choking and was on his way to the emergency room. A parent rushed Almond across the northeastern corner of the state to the hospital, where his son eventually resumed breathing and recovered. Within a few weeks his wife had given birth to a daughter, their second child. The domestic stresses continued; a few months later his marriage broke up. Almond decided midway through the spring that he no longer wanted to teach in Salem, and a substitute teacher took his place for the rest of the year. This also meant that Almond could not coach track. He missed the runners he had brought up, especially the upcoming senior class: Deirdre Clary, Berly Kenst, Veronica Waite, Ryan Griffith, Mike Overholser, Justin "Stogus" Roberts, Aiman Scullion, Jason Stewart, and Paul and Joe Shivers. But he left all the same.

Almond's classroom door was once covered in newspaper clippings about Salem High School runners, but these and the former coach's other decorations were removed. There remained one trace of Almond's brief days at SHS: a magnet stuck on the wall outside his room that read "Keep the faith. Finish the race." Mike Almond now manages a Second Sole running supply store in the Akron area, where he can stay immersed in the sport he loves and see any of his runners who stop by to visit.

Without Almond, the Quakers feared that Salem's running program would fall from the elite. But Rick Wilson, the former assistant coach, and Mary, his wife, took over the boys' and girls' teams, respectively. The team reloaded with five bright–eyed, fleet–footed freshmen: J.D. Winkler, Brandon Floor, Jason Floor (Brandon's brother), Ted Yuhaniak (Tommy's brother) and Brian Shivers (Joe's brother). Salem also gained senior Mike Downs, who came out to stay in shape for track but soon realized he was one of the fastest boys on the team. Every day he ran, his interest in the sport grew. Soon he was running twelve–milers and competing with Mike Overholser for the fourth spot on the team. Salem seemed like a sure bet to repeat its state championship, and the boys even aspired to the prestigious Nike Team Nationals meet.

But the season turned sour even before the first meet, when Paul got a stress fracture in late July. He rowed, swam, and lifted, but none of those were substitutes for the sixty and seventy mile weeks his teammates were running. He recovered in time for the Great American Cross Country Festival in North Carolina, a meet that drew elite teams from over twenty states. Nonetheless, the Quakers on the whole performed poorly at their race, finishing fourteenth in a meet where they had hoped to make a name for themselves, and the next few races were even worse. Mike Downs, the team's new recruit, fell victim to Achilles troubles and was forced to sit out indefinitely. The competition in D II had gotten tougher, as well – Walsh was not even Salem's greatest rival. Peninsula Woodridge, a young team from Salem's region, cleanly beat the Quakers in a midseason meet. Akron St. Vincent–St. Mary's defeated Salem, too.

The boys tried to rationalize losing not only to a school from Ohio, not only to a school in Division II, but to two such schools. Downs, Salem's fourth man, did not run in either of those meets, but the team was still badly shaken. Wilson struggled to maintain his trademark positive attitude, but it seemed like the Salem boys had missed their chance to win again. In the summer the pundits had called Salem a sure bet to repeat, but now nobody favored Salem for the State title.

Meanwhile the girls' team, under the guidance of Mary Wilson, was gradually upstaging the boys. Seniors Deirdre, Berly, and Veronica led the small but passionate group through excellent performances week after week in key meets. Erin Murphy, Alexis Thorne, Kathy Ellis, Liz and Lauren Shivers (Mark's daughters), Sarah Yerkey, and Kristin Pihlgren quietly turned the girls' team into an unflappable squad of competitors. Their goal was to advance to State, but it was becoming increasingly apparent that the young ladies could anticipate more than just an appearance at the championship meet.

The Regional meet came. The boys' team consisted of Aiman – now a true frontrunner after finally quitting soccer, Paul – whose intense summer cross–training had helped him to regain his second–place spot on the team, Gorby – still doubting himself but still tough and fast, Mike Downs – still injured, but forcing himself to sacrifice for the team of which he had become a part, Mike Overholser – who had sat out track season with an ankle injury and begun the summer hopelessly out of shape, but worked himself into as good a runner as ever, Ryan Griffith – still playful but no longer inexperienced, and Justin Roberts – having set his sights on varsity in his senior year, and let nothing stand in his way. Joe again served as alternate after two decisive late–season losses to Justin and Ryan. This year, however, Joe resolved to appreciate his role and help his team however he could. Wilson had named him and Paul co–captains, and the two

Shiverses had worked to prepare their teammates for a Regional victory.

That victory did not come. The Quakers placed third behind Woodridge and St. V's after a Boardman Regional race in which (for the fourth year in a row) nearly all of them ran badly. Walsh was ousted by the perennial dark horse Aurora, failing to make the State Meet just one year after a second–place finish. The forty point difference between Salem and the Regional Champion Woodridge seemed insurmountable. The girls won their meet, so for the first time in Salem's history both teams earned berths at Scioto Downs. The girls were thrilled; the boys were apoplectic.

A loss was out of the question. Mike Overholser promised again and again that he simply would not leave Columbus without a state championship. The boys did more soul–searching, and by the middle of the week Wilson had persuaded them they had a chance at Saturday's meet. On Tuesday, Paul got the flu. On Wednesday, he was on an IV for the duration of the day. And on Friday morning, just before the traditional pre–State mass at St. Paul's Church, his and Joe's grandmother died.

Margaret Vietmeier Shivers was mother to eleven and grandmother to twenty–five. Five of those grandchildren (Paul, Joe, Brian, Liz, and Lauren) ran cross country for SHS in 2005. On Thursday, the night before she died, she had said to Liz, "You're running in that race on Saturday. You're going to win it." The meet took on another dimension.

Saturday morning, November 5, 2005, the girls did win that race. Liz and Lauren took 23rd and 43rd place, respectively, to help their team edge Kettering Alter and earn Salem High School's first championship in any girls' sport. Sarah Yerkey had the breakout race of the day. Her little brother Blair had died less than a month before, and her teammates had all grieved with her and her family. From the mourning came a kind of resolve, and the girls had, in effect, dedicated the season to him. They felt good about their victory on many levels as they prepared to cheer on the boys.

The boys needed to win, and they were not going to let any last–minute problems stop them. Mike Downs was coming off an injury and had had little training since the middle of the season. Aiman and Mike had stayed up till 3am the previous night for reasons no one on the team could understand. Patrick and Ryan decided to go for a morning swim, shocking their muscles with alternating bouts in the pool and hot tub. And not only had Paul run just three times all week due to his illness, but he had lost his grandmother the day before.

Joe watched from the infield of the Scioto Downs racetrack as the gun fired and his teammates started sprinting. The boys looked pretty good throughout the race, but not great. Aiman made a push for the win during the second mile, but came up short in the strong winds. He fell back into the teens. Paul got off to a slow start, and was failing to make up ground on the front pack. Patrick was running solid, but Mike and Mike were struggling. Aiman finished 11th, Paul and Patrick 18th and 19th, and Overholser and Downs 58th and 60th. As Joe approached the finish chute to greet the finishing racers, he was joined by his Mike Almond. Despite being neither a coach, nor an official, nor a reporter, Almond had somehow snuck into the race area to watch the Salem teams run. He would not have missed it.

Half an hour later, the boys sat in their now–customary place behind the officials' trailer and watched as Almond and Wilson checked the results. Paul worried; although Woodridge had run poorly, St. V's might have stolen the top spot …then he saw Almond and Wilson sprinting towards the team, clutching each other and laughing. "First place! We won!"

There followed a celebration unprecedented in the team's history. Mike Overholser cried with joy…for the next hour. Grandma Shivers' deathbed prediction had been fulfilled. They had done it. The boys had won State for the second year in a row. For only the third time in OHSAA Cross Country history, the same high school's boys' and girls' teams had won the State Meet. Almond had re–awakened a cross country power, and Wilson seemed ready to carry on the tradition.

Acknowledgements

First, we thank Bill Jelen, our patient and helpful publisher, without whom this book would not have been written; Lee Galada, Tessa Sean Hershberger, Joshua Matthew Moorhead, and Ashley Shawntel, for taking the Fresh Writers Books boat on its maiden voyage; and Bridget O'Dwyer, for accompanying us on our first foray into literature. To paraphrase the great Jim Dombroski, this book was fun.

We would like to thank everyone who has contributed to this book in some way, especially Tom Patton, Joe Rottenborn, Joe Shivers, Madeline Shivers, and Robert Viencek for proofreading the manuscript; Greg Steffey, for providing us with notes from the 2003 postseason; our fathers, Joe and Paul Shivers, for encouraging us to enter the Fresh Writers Book competition in the first place; Rick Reilly, Marc Bloom, and John Feinstein, who set standards of sportswriting we aspire to uphold; all of our writing teachers over the years, Clara Tolson, Nancy Clapsadle, Patti Bauman, Sandy Collopy, Marjorie Shivers, Sally Fieldhouse, JoAnn Barto, Deanna Wilson, Larry Breckenridge, Jim Lantz, Jean Esposito, Melanie Dye, Steve Shurtleff, Sarah Weir, Pat Potter, Connie Ridgeway, Amie Cochran, Tami Comm, Kerry Ramunno, Bill Taylor, Mary Beth Shivers, Carol Hrvatin, Judy Herron, and Robert Viencek.

This is the story of the Salem High School Cross Country team, and we thank all of our teammates through the years: Rebecca Keen, Ronda Williams, Carla Gbur, Erica Davis, Brandi Sauerwein, Kim Yakovich, Gabby Folger,Lori Singer,

Ashley Shea, Erica Linam, Kristin Pihlgren, Kathy Ellis, Lauren Shivers, Alexis Thorne, Jim Dombroski, Shane Harding, Isaac Ieropoli, Alex Barnett, Alex Hoopes, Andrew Bender, Jeff Linam, Tyler Bender, Mike Downs, Connor Shivers, Andy Thompson, Brandon Floor, Jason Floor, Brian Shivers, J.D. Winkler, and Ted Yuhaniak; especially those who ran during the 2003 and 2004 seasons: Allyson Pasqual, Jenna Cramer, Jen Teal, Ali Calvin,

Deirdre Clary, Berly Kenst, Kayla Niederhiser, Veronica Waite, Erin Murphy, Liz Shivers, Cassie Tanley, Sarah Yerkey, Jason Naylor, Josh Matthews, Lance Murphy, Isaac Newton, Matt Yanek, Ryan Griffith, Mike Overholser, Justin Roberts, Aiman Scullion, Jason Stewart, Patrick Gorby, Tom Yuhaniak, and Erik Cibula. Thanks to Coaches Mike Almond, Rick Wilson, and Russ Hopple for leading us down the road.

Thanks to our track other track and cross country coaches, Todd Huda, Jerry Rabell, Matt Ziegler, Ralph Hoehn, Jim Shivers, and Dave Direnzo, for helping us on the way; Salem Parks crew, for keeping our home course well–groomed; the X–tra Mile Club, for spoiling us with jerseys, heart rate monitors, and an abundance of food; the staff of Silverio Physical Therapy, who have kept us on our feet; the Salem School Board and administration, for fighting so that we could run.

Thanks to our mothers, Madeline and Laura Shivers, for keeping us focused and optimistic; and our siblings, Brian and Luke, Lydia, Anthony, and Maria for cheering at our cross country meets and encouraging us in this latest venture. Thanks for the love.

Chronology

July 2002 – Michael Almond holds his first practice as head coach of the Salem Cross Country Team.

October 12, 2002 – For the first time in nine years, both the Salem boys' and girls' teams finish well enough in Districts to qualify for the Regional Meet.

October 19, 2002 – The Salem boys finish dead last in the Regional Meet. Shane Harding qualifies for State (held on October 26) and finishes 30th overall.

October 18, 2003 – The Salem boys win their District on a tiebreaker with Cardinal Mooney.

October 25, 2003 – The initial results of the Regional Meet show Salem beating Cardinal Mooney for the sixth and final State Meet berth. However, after reviewing the race, officials rule that Salem in fact lost to Mooney.

October 31, 2003 – The Salem School District seeks a temporary restraining order against the OHSAA, thereby allowing the cross country team to race at State. The case is thrown out of the Franklin County Court.

November 1, 2003 – The team rides to Columbus, where they learn that the school district's request for a temporary restraining order has been granted by the Columbiana County Court.

November 2, 2003 – Salem finishes third overall in the D II State Championships. Paul and Patrick finish with All-Ohio Honors.

November 12, 2003 – The Columbiana Country Court rules against the Salem City School District's attempt for a permanent injunction against the OHSAA. The team is stripped of its third place finish.

May 29, 2004 – Aiman qualifies for the State Track Championships in the 3200m. The 4x800m team, including Patrick and Lance, finishes a disappointing 7th.

October 23, 2004 – Led by Aiman's first-place finish, the Salem boys easily defend their District Title.

October 30, 2004 – In an upset, Walsh Jesuit beats Salem to win the Regional Meet.

November 4, 2004 – The Salem Boys' Cross Country Team wins the Division II State Championship by the second-largest margin on record.

Spring 2005 – Michael Almond resigns from teaching and coaching at Salem.

November 5, 2005 – Under new Head Coaches Rick and Mary Wilson, both the girls' and boys' teams win State Titles.

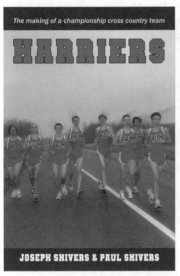

HARRIERS

Harriers is the story of the quest for a cross country state championship, as told by two members of the team. The book captures the feelings and moods of the high school runner. It yields insights about hard work and disappointment, about trust and relationships. It rings true with the team's hopes, dreams, disappointments, and triumphs. Harriers is a great recruiting tool for the prospective high school runner. For adult runners, Harriers will bring back a flood of memories from your days as a high school runner.

From left: Coach Rick Wilson, Josh Matthews, Matt Yanek, Isaac Newton, Patrick Gorby, Aiman Scullion, Paul Shivers, Mike Overholser, Ryan Griffith, Joe Shivers, Coach Mike Almond

FreshWriters

Fresh Writers Books
PO Box 82, Uniontown OH 44685